I0168619

Washington's Early Campaigns

Washington's Early Campaigns

The French Post Expedition,
Great Meadows and
Braddock's Defeat
—including Braddock's Orderly Books—

James Hadden

LEONAUR

Washington's Early Campaigns
by James Hadden

First published under the titles
Washington's Expeditions and
Braddock's Orderly Book

Leonaur is an imprint of Oakpast Ltd

Copyright in this form © 2008 Oakpast Ltd

ISBN: 978-1-84677-628-1 (hardcover)
ISBN: 978-1-84677-627-4 (softcover)

http://www.leonaur.com

Publisher's Notes

In the interests of authenticity, the spellings, grammar and place names
used have been retained from the original editions.

The opinions of the authors represent a view of events in which he
was a participant related from his own perspective,
as such the text is relevant as an historical document.

The views expressed in this book are not necessarily
those of the publisher.

Contents

Washington's Expeditions

James Hadden

THE GREAT MEADOWS WITH FORT NECESSITY OUTLINED IN THE CENTRE
- 1904

Contents

Preface

In presenting this narrative of the expeditions of Lieutenant Colonel George Washington and Major General Edward Braddock to the public it is with the belief that a short and comprehensive relation of these two important events in the history of our country will prove both interesting and instructive.

These expeditions were the initiatives of a great struggle between two great powers to decide whether America was to be an appendage of France or to become the land of an English-speaking race.

The great Mississippi valley, a region vast enough and fertile enough to feed the inhabitants of the world, was a goal far more to be desired than for which the armies of the nations had ever before contended.

Not only this, but these expeditions schooled the colonists in the arts of war and gave them that confidence in their prowess that enabled them later successfully to throw off the yoke of oppression and establish a new nation which is now attracting the wonder and admiration of the civilized world.

Washington's Mission to the French Posts at the Head of the Allegheny River, 1753.

More than a century had elapsed after the discovery of this continent by the Cabots before the first English settlement was established in America, and one hundred and forty years more had rolled away before settlements were attempted west of the Allegheny Mountains. Thus for two hundred and fifty years after having gained possession by discovery had England been content to colonize only the American seaboard.

The French had made settlements on the St. Lawrence, and by the last half of the seventeenth century had pushed their way along the shores of the great lakes, and by the middle of the eighteenth century had explored the country from the lakes on the north to the gulf on the south and from the Alleghenies on the east to the Mississippi on the west, and had established their trading posts and their missions.

Although a lucrative business had been carried on for some years by Pennsylvania, Maryland and Virginia fur traders with the Indians of the Ohio Valley, no systematic effort on the part of the English colonists had been made to establish settlements west of the Allegheny Mountains until 1748, when Thomas Lee, president of the Virginia Council, associated with himself twelve other gentlemen, among whom were Gov. Robert Dinwiddie, Lawrence and Augustine Washington—brothers of George

Washington, and Mr. John Hamburg, a wealthy merchant of London. This company was to be known as the Ohio Company, and a royal grant was obtained in March, 1749, for a tract of five hundred thousand acres of land lying on the south side of the Ohio and between the Monongahela and the Kanawha rivers, with privilege to embrace a portion of land on the north side if deemed expedient. Two hundred thousand acres were to be selected immediately, the whole to be exempt from quit rent for ten years, the company agreeing to seat one hundred families on the same within seven years, and at their own expense to build a fort and maintain a garrison sufficient to protect the settlement.

Christopher Gist was employed as the agent for this Ohio Company to select the lands and to conciliate the Indians. With these objects in view he left his home on the banks of the Yodkin, near the boundary line between Virginia and North Carolina, in the fall of 1749, and ascended the Potomac to the mouth of Wills Creek. From here, on the thirty-first of October, he proceeded to where Bedford is now located, and from thence to the Forks of the Ohio. At Logstown, about sixteen miles below the Forks, a conference was held with Tanacharison, a Seneca chief of great note, he being head Sachem of the mixed tribes, which had migrated to the Ohio and its tributaries. He was generally surnamed the Half-King, being subordinate to the Iroquois Confederacy, and was a man of considerable intelligence. After the usual formalities and the delivery of my presents in securing the friendship of the Indians, Gist passed on down the Ohio River to within fifteen miles of the and thence by a circuitous route he returned to Virginia in 1751.

In 1750 the Ohio Company built a small storehouse on the site once occupied by the Shawanee town Cainctucuc on the west side of Will's Creek where that stream empties into the Potomac River and where the city of Cumberland now stands, and the following year Colonel Thomas Cresap, who then lived at Shawanee Old Town, was employed to open out a road from Will's Creek to the mouth of the Monongahela. He wisely selected for his assistant a Delaware Indian by the name of Nemacolin, whose residence was at the mouth of Nemacolin's Creek, now known as Dunlap's Creek, on the Monongahela River. Beginning at the terminus of the road already made, to the storehouse at Will's Creek, they followed an old trail worn by the foot of the red man centuries before the pale face beheld the outlines of a new continent. Running westward until reaching the crest of Laurel Hill this road turned abruptly northward along the crest of the mountain and descended the western slope, where it joined the old Catawba Trail what is now known as the Mt. Braddock farm. From this point northward this road was, with few deviations, identical with the above mentioned trail, crossing the Youghiogheny River a short distance below the present town of New Haven, passing to the west of the location of Mount Pleasant, and when reaching a point to the west of the location of Greensburg it deflected to the west and on to the Forks of the Ohio. From the fact that Nemacolin was employed on the improvement of the trail it received the name of Nemacolin's Trail, which name it retained until Braddock's army passed over it, since which it has been known as Braddock's Road.

Gist made a second survey for the Ohio Company in 1752, this time passing over the Nemacolin Trail and crossing the Monongahela below where McKeesport now stands. Returning, he crossed the Monongahela at the mouth of Nemacolin Creek, where he met his old Indian friend, who proposed the following question: "If the French claim all the land north of the Ohio, and the English all on the south, where do the Indians lands lie?" This question went unanswered.

Gist had selected for himself twenty-five hundred acres of land at the foot of Laurel Hill, considering this within the Ohio Company's grant, and in 1753 he here established a small settlement consisting of eleven families. He built his cabin near a fine spring and within a few rods of the exact geographical centre of Fayette County. He was the second settler within the bounds of what is now Fayette County, Wendell Brown having preceded him by one year.

MAJOR GEORGE WASHINGTON - 1754

In 1753 the French began active measures to secure the Ohio valley by the force of arms by erecting a cordon of forts to extend from Lake Erie down the Allegheny and Ohio rivers. This news soon reached the ears of the governor of Virginia, who in the fall of the same year determined to dispatch a messenger to demand of the French an explanation of their design and warn them off.

George Washington, then in his twenty-second year, was commissioned by Governor Dinwiddie as a special envoy to proceed to the headwaters of the Allegheny and deliver the message to General St. Pierre, the French commander. He started out on his journey October thirtieth, the day or the day after he had received his credentials, and arrived at Will's Creek November fourteenth. Here he secured the services of Christopher Gist as guide, John Davidson as Indian interpreter, Captain Jacob Van Braam as French interpreter; Curram and McQuire, Indian traders, and Stewart and Jenkins—these four as servitors.

From here they followed the Nemacolin Trail, passing Gist's new settlement, and after seven days reached Frazier's trading post at the mouth of Turtle Creek, on the Monongahela River. Passing on down they arrived at Logstown, about sixteen miles below the Forks, after sunset November twenty-fourth. Here a consultation was held with Tanacharison, the Half-King; Monacatootha, the next in command, and other friendly Indians of the mixed tribes, some of which Washington engaged to accompany him to Venango, the advance post of the French. Here they arrived December fourth, and found the French flag flying over the log house from which Frazier, the English trader, had been driven and which was now occupied by Joncaire, who referred Washington to the commanding officer, whose headquarters were at Le Boeuf, the fort lately built a short distance above on French Creek. Here he was courteously received by Legardeur de St. Pierre, who promised to forward his message to the governor-general of Canada, and refused to discuss the great questions involving the remonstrance of Virginia, but stated that he would m the meantime hold his position to the best of his ability, and intended, further, to eject every Englishman from the Ohio valley.

His mission fulfilled, Washington, after much delay, started back, and becoming impatient of the company he and Gist alone concluded to strike out on foot across the country. After much fatigue and suffering, being shot at by a treacherous Indian and nearly lost in the Allegheny River, they reached Frazier's house once more. They left Frazier's on January 1, 1754, and reached Gist's plantation on January second. Here they procured horses and pressed on, reaching Wills Creek on the sixth. Washington spent the night with Gist, and met seventeen horses loaded with material and stores for the fort at the Forks of the Ohio, and the day after some families going out to settle. The Ohio Company, having determined to build their fort at the Forks and to establish trading posts at Frazier's and elsewhere, were proceeding energetically toward me accomplishment of these objects. He delivered the message of Saint Pierre and made a full report of his journey to the governor at Williamsburg on the sixteenth of January; thus Washington's first important public service was accomplished.

Before Washington had returned from his mission to the French forts the Ohio Company had appealed to Governor Dinwiddie for military protection at their fort already begun at the Forks, in compliance with which, early in January of 1754, Wm. Trent, an explorer, who at this time was engaged in erecting a strong log storehouse at the mouth of Redstone Creek on the Monongahela River for the Ohio Company—this being the next storehouse west of that already built at Wills Creek, was commissioned as captain, John Frazier, before mentioned, as lieutenant, and Edward Ward, appointed as ensign, were authorized to raise a company of militia of one hundred men, proceed to the Forks and finish and garrison the fort already begun.

Trent proceeded by Nemacolin's Trail as far as Gist's plantation, and from thence to the mouth of Redstone, where after finishing the Hangard he returned to Wills Creek, leaving Ensign Ward in command to proceed to the Forks, at which place he arrived on the seventeenth of February. Here with Gist and George Croghan they proceeded to finish the fort, which was supplied with ten four-pound field pieces and eighty barrels of powder and a supply of small arms.

The French Descend the Allegheny in Considerable Force.

Everything seemed quiet until the Allegheny, freed from ice, opened in the spring. On April thirteenth Ensign Ward received notice that the French were descending the river in considerable force.

The following day he dispatched a letter to Captain Trent at Wills Creek, and went directly himself to Lieutenant Frazier at Turtle Creek, who replied that he could not leave his work, as by doing so he would lose shillings for every pence he would receive for his services. The following morning Ensign Ward sent for the Half-King and one of his chiefs named Serreneatta, and set to work to finish the stockade. They had the last gate erected before the French appeared.

On the seventeenth Contrecoeur appeared before the fort with three hundred wooden canoes and sixty bateaux with four men to each, eighteen pieces of cannon, three of which were nine-pounders. A landing was made a small distance from the fort, and Le Mercier was sent to demand a surrender of the fort. Looking at his watch, which indicated two o'clock, he demanded that an answer be delivered at the French camp in writing within one hour. Ensign Ward spent half of this hour in consulting with the Half-King, who advised him to acquaint the French commander that he was not an officer of rank, nor invested with power to answer his demand, and to request him to await the arrival of the principal commander. Contrecoeur was inflexible, and demanded an answer that instant.

Ward saw the French to number about a thousand, and his own force being forty-one in all—only thirty-three of which were soldiers, he surrendered, with liberty to march off with everything belonging thereto by twelve o clock the next day. He encamped within three hundred yards of the fort with a party of friendly Indians. The French commander sent for him to supper and made many inquiries as to the intention of the English, but Ward refused to impart the desired information. The commander then tried to buy some carpenter tools, which Ward refused to sell.

The following morning Ensign Ward received a speech from Half-King to the governor and proceeded with all his men to Redstone, where he arrived in two days, and from there to Will's Creek, where he arrived on the twenty-second and met Colonel Washington on his way to the Forks.

The French immediately completed the stockade evacuated by Ensign Ward and named it Fort Duquesne in donor of the governor-general of Canada.

The reply of the French general, Saint Pierre, together with the information received from Washington, convinced Governor Dinwiddie that inaction on his part would lose to the English the whole valley of the Ohio.

Washington is Commissioned Major and Ordered Against the French

He therefore commissioned Washington as major, with authority to enlist one hundred and fifty men and proceed to the Forks of the Ohio to finish the fort already begun, to make prisoners and to kill or destroy all who interrupted the English settlement. This commission was soon raised to that of lieutenant-colonel, and the number of men increased to three hundred, to be divided into six companies. Enlistments were encouraged by a royal grant of two hundred thousand acres of land, to be divided among them. Colonel Joshua Fry, an English gentleman, was appointed to command the whole, and was to follow with the artillery to be conveyed up the Potomac. The first intention was to make a wagon road from Will's Creek, to which point the Ohio Company had already opened a road, to the mouth of Redstone, and there erect a fort; thence, when re-enforced, to proceed against the French at the Forks. With these objects in view Washington started from Alexandria, Virginia, April 2, 1754, with two companies, amounting to one hundred and fifty men, and having been joined on the route by a detachment under Captain Adam Stephens, arrived at Will's Creek, April twentieth. and two days later Ensign Ward arrived with the intelligence of the surrender of the works at the Forks of the Ohio.

From here sixty men were sent forward to widen the Nemacolin Trail, and April twenty-ninth the army moved from Will's Creek, and by the ninth of May were encamped at the Little Meadows, a distance of twenty miles. Here Washington received information that Contrecoeur had been re-enforced with eight hundred men, and expresses were immediately sent to the governors of Pennsylvania, Virginia and Maryland requesting reenforcements. and after consultation with his brother officers decided to advance. Castleman Creek was two miles west of Little Meadows, and here more than two days were spent in bridging the stream; this was named the Little Crossings. On the eighteenth the Youghiogheny River was reached, seventeen miles west of the Little Crossings, and although the army was enabled to cross without bridging, this place was named the Big Crossings.

While the army lay here several days Washington, with Lieutenant West, three soldiers and an Indian descended the river in a canoe to ascertain if it was navigable for me transportation of the artillery, which they had been obliged to drag by hand since leaving Wills Creek. This journey ended in disappointment at the Falls, a distance of thirty miles from the Great Crossings. Scarcely had Washington returned from his journey to the falls when a messenger arrived from his old friend, the Half-King, that a detachment of French was marching toward him with a determination to make an attack, and that he (the Half-King) would be on in five days to hold a council. Washington thereupon hastened to the Great Meadows, a distance of about fifty-one miles west of Wills Creek, reaching this place on the twenty-fourth of May, and here he again received intelligence that the French were on their way to meet him. A halt was made and a stockade erected, and by clearing away the brush and undergrowth, prepared, as he said, "a most charming field for an encounter."

A scouting party was sent out on wagon horses to reconnoitre, but returned without having seen an enemy. The same evening the Half-King's warning was confirmed by a trader, who told that the French were at the crossing of the Youghiogheny, eighteen miles distant from the Big Crossings, and known as Stewart's Crossing, as William Stewart lived near that place in 1753 and part of 1754, and was driven out by the French.

About two o'clock in the night an alarm was given. The sentries fired upon what they mistook to be prowling foes; the troops sprang to arms and remained on the alert until daybreak. Not an enemy was to be seen. The roll was called and six men were missing, having deserted.

On May twenty-seventh Mr. Gist came in and reported that La Force, with a detachment of about fifty men, had been seen at his place, about fifteen miles distant, and that he had just come upon their tracks within five miles of the camp, whereupon Washington sent a detachment of seventy-five men in pursuit of him and his band, but the scouts returned without having discovered the enemy.

Rock Fort Where the half-king was encamped

The Half-King Joins Washington

Between eight and nine o clock that same night a messenger arrived from Half-King, who with his followers was then encamped at the Big Rock, about six miles off, with the information that he had tracked two men who were out as scouts, and was satisfied that the whole force was in ambush nearby. Washington, fearing a stratagem, left a strong guard to protect the baggage, and with a detachment of forty men set out before ten o'clock to join the Indian allies. They groped their way along the footpath in a heavy rain and murky darkness, so that it was nearly sunrise when they reached the encampment of Half-King. From here the Half-King and his associate *sachem*, Scarooyada or Monacatootha, conducted Washington to the tracks which had been discovered. Upon these he put two of his Indians, who followed them up like hounds and brought back word that they had traced them to a low bottom surrounded by rocks and trees, where the French were encamped, having built a few cabins for shelter from the rain.

A plan of attack was now determined upon to come upon them by surprise. Washington and his men formed on the right, Half-King and his men on the left, and with ghost-like silence they advanced to the brow of the ledge of rocks beneath which the French were encamped. Washington was in the advance, and as the French caught sight of him they flew to arms. A sharp fire ensued, which lasted for fifteen minutes, when the French gave way and ran. They were soon overtaken, and twenty-one

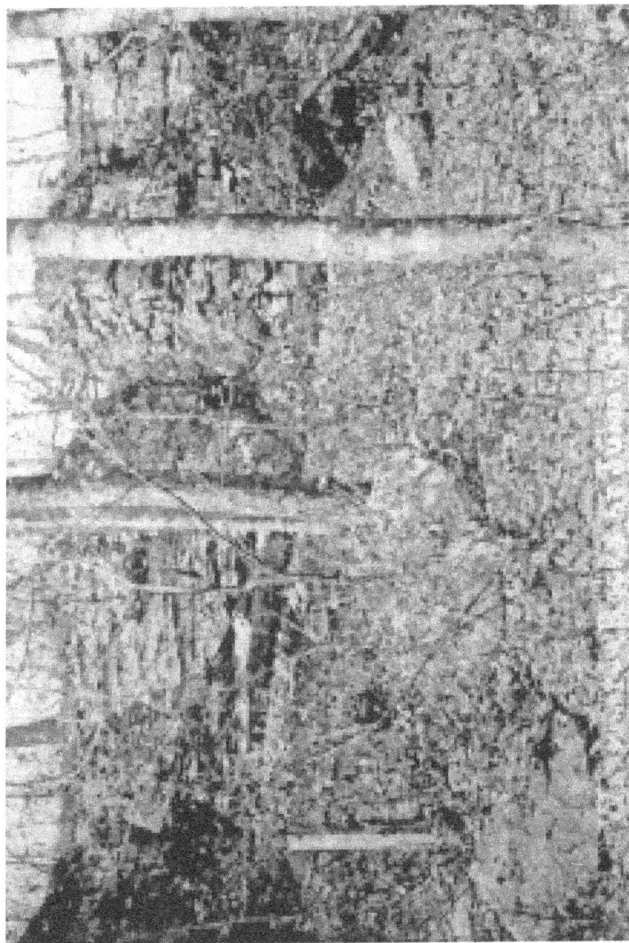

LEDGE OF ROCKS FROM WHICH WASHINGTON FIRED ON THE FRENCH

prisoners taken. Washington's men on the right received the fire of the enemy. One man was killed and three wounded near Washington, the Indians sustaining no loss. The French had ten killed and one wounded. One, a bare-footed Canadian, named Mouceau, escaped and carried the tidings of the defeat to the Forks. Monsieur Jumonville, their commander, was shot through the head at the first fire, and his fate has been made the subject of lamentation in prose and verse. The Indians soon scalped the dead, and would have killed and scalped the prisoners had not Washington prevented them.

This battle, fought at daybreak on the morning of May 28, 1754, was the first in which Washington ever took a part; it was the initial battle which lost to the French so much of her possessions on American soil, and as Francis Parkman tersely put it,

"in it was fired the shot that was heard around the world."

Washington, in writing of this occasion, said:

"And believe me, the whistling of the bullets had a most charming sound."

Jumonville was a native of Picardy, one of the old French provinces bordering on the English Channel. His name was N. Coulon de Jumonville, and he was at the age of twenty-nine years, therefore seven years the senior of Washington. Early in life he came to Canada and married. He left a widow and one daughter. In 1755, one year after his death, the widow was pensioned in a small sum, and in 1775 the daughter, then grown to womanhood, took the veil as Charlotte Amiable.

Of the twenty-one prisoners taken at this engagement the two most important were an officer of some consequence, named Drouillion, and the subtle and redoubtable La Force. As Washington considered the latter an arch mischief-maker, who had made considerable trouble at Venango the year previous, he now rejoiced to have him within his power. The prisoners were conducted to the camp at the Great Meadows, and from there, on the following day, were sent under a strong escort to Governor Dinwiddie, who was at Winchester, Virginia. They were treated with great courtesy by Washington, who furnished Drouillion and La Force with clothing from his own scanty stock, and at their request gave them letters to the governor bespeaking for them the "respect and favour due their character and personal merit."

The Half-King was now fully aroused. He sent the scalps of the Frenchmen slain in the late skirmish, accompanied with black *wampum* and hatchets, to all his allies, summoning them to take up arms and join him at Redstone Creek, "for their brothers, the English, had now begun in earnest." He went off to his home, promising to send down the river for all the Mingoes and Shawanees and to be back at the camp on the thirteenth with thirty or forty warriors accompanied by their wives and children. To assist him in the transportation of his people and their effects thirty men were detached, and twenty horses.

A pile of stones and a rude cross marked the grave of Jumonville until July 4th, 1908, when a tablet was erected bearing the following inscription:

Here lie the mortal remains
of
N. Coulon de Jumonville,
who in command of thirty-three French regulars, was surprised and killed in an engagement with Major George Washington, in command of forty provincial troops, and Tannacharison, the Half-King in command of a company of friendly Indians, on May 28, 1754.
This action was the first conflict at arms between the French and English for supremacy in the Mississippi valley.
Erected July 4th, 1908, under the auspices of the Centennial Committee of 1904.

Washington's situation now was extremely perilous. Contrecoeur had finished the fort from which Ward had been driven. He had already nearly one thousand men with him, and re-enforcements and Indian allies were on their way to join him. Messengers sent by Jumonville previous to the late affray apprised him of the weakness of the encampment at the Great Meadows.

Washington lost no time in enlarging the entrenchments and erecting palisades. He wrote to Colonel Fry, who lay sick at Wills Creek, having been seriously injured by his horse falling on him, urging immediate re-enforcements, but at the same time declaring his resolution to "fight with unequal numbers rather than give up one inch of what he had gained." The Half-King and Queen Aliquippa and twenty-five or thirty families, making in all eighty to one hundred Indians, arrived at the Great Meadows on June first.

Colonel Fry died on the thirty-first of May, a few days after the accident, and Major Muse took command and joined Washington, where he arrived on the ninth of June with the residue of the Virginia regiment and nine swivel guns, powder and balls. Major Muse had served with Lawrence Washington in the campaign of the West Indies, and had been with him m the attack on Carthagena. He had been Washington's instructor three years before in the manual of arms, and was now acting as quartermaster. By the death of Colonel Fry the chief command devolved upon Major Washington, who was commissioned lieutenant-colonel on June fourth.

Captain James Mackaye, with an independent company of the royal army, composed of one hundred men from South Carolina, joined Washington on the tenth of June, bringing with him beeves, five days' allowance of flour and some ammunition, but no cannon, as was expected. Captain Mackaye bearing a king's commission, could not receive orders from a provincial colonel, and camped separate from Washington's forces; neither would his men do work on the road, as it was not incumbent upon them as king's soldiers to perform such menial service. The force now encamped at the Great Meadows numbered about four hundred men.

JUMONVILLE'S GRAVE

Leaving Captain Mackaye with one company to guard the fort, to thus avoid mutiny and a conflict of authority, Washington and the rest of the force, on the sixteenth of June, pushed on over Laurel Hill, cutting the road with extreme labour, to Gist's plantation—a distance of about thirteen miles, consuming two weeks in the work, taking with him some wagons and the swivels.

On June twenty-seventh a detachment of seventy men under command of Captain Lewis was sent forward to clear the road from Gist's to the mouth of Redstone. Ahead of this was sent a party under Captain Polson, who were to reconnoitre. Meanwhile Washington completed his movements to Gist's.

Washington Retreats to the Great Meadows and Strengthens Fort Necessity

On the twenty-ninth a council of war was held at Gist's at which it was determined to concentrate all the forces at this point, where some entrenchments had been already thrown up, with a view of making a stand. This entrenchment was near Gist's Indian's hut and a fine spring, and within fifty rods of the geographical centre of Fayette County.

Captains Lewis and Polson were called in, and Captain Mackaye and his company were sent for. They all came, but upon receiving later news of the superior force of the French it was apparent that a stand here was inexpedient and that they should fall back as far as Will's Creek and await re-enforcements. The private baggage was left behind, and the horses of the officers were laden with ammunition and public stores. The soldiers of the Virginia regiment dragged the nine swivels by hand, the members of the independent company looking on and offering no aid. They reached the Great Meadows on the first day of July. Here the men were so exhausted by their labours and lack of nourishment that they could not draw their swivels nor carry their baggage on their backs any farther. They had been eight days without bread. They had milch cows for beef, but had no salt with which to season it, nor were the supplies which had been left at the stockade adequate to sustain the march. It was thought best, therefore, to here await both the supplies and re-enforcements, having now but two poor teams and a few equally poor pack horses.

Washington immediately set his men to work to strengthen the fortifications, and under the supervision of Captain Stobo a ditch and additional dimensions and strength were given to the fort, which was now given the name of Fort Necessity on account of the extreme need of the troops.

Hearing of the arrival at Alexandria of two independent companies from New York some days before it was supposed that they might by this time have arrived at Wills Creek, and a messenger was dispatched to urge them up. Horses were hired to go to Wills Creek for more ammunition and provisions, Gist endeavouring to have the artillery hauled out by Pennsylvania teams. It was ascertained that the two independent companies from New York and the one from North Carolina would fail to arrive until too late, and they only reached Wills Creek after the surrender of Fort Necessity. No artillery came in time, only ten of the thirty four-pound cannon and carriages which had been sent from England reaching Wills Creek until too late.

Besides the Indians already mentioned as crowding into the fort, many of the settlers with their families sought protection under the English arms. The warriors expected and promised by the Half-King from the Muskingum and Miami countries failed to join Washington.

From the time news reached Fort Duquesne of the defeat of Jumonville the greatest activity prevailed. On the twenty-eighth of June, just one month after that affair, a force of five hundred French and one hundred Indians, afterwards augmented to four hundred, left Fort Duquesne under command of M. Coulon de Villiers, a half-brother to Jumonville, who sought the command as a special favour to enable him, as he termed it, to avenge the "assassination" of his kinsman.

De Villiers passed up the Monongahela on the thirtieth of June, and then moved on to Gist's settlement, a distance of about sixteen miles, reaching the place early the morning of the second of July. Opening fire upon the rude half-finished fort, and receiving no response, he found the place deserted. He thereupon prepared to return to Fort Duquesne, when a deserter arrived from Fort Necessity, who revealed the whereabouts and wretched condition of Washington's forces. He concluded to press on in pursuit of the English. He ascended the mountain by the road just opened by Washington, passed within five hundred yards of where his half-brother had fallen a little over a month before, and came within sight of Fort Necessity, after a rainy night, early on the morning of the third of July. He immediately delivered the first fire from the woods, at a distance of four or five hundred yards. The first position taken by the French was in the north-west, but afterwards they took position on the east and south-east, near the fort. Washington formed his men on the south, in the meadow outside the fort, in order to draw the enemy into an open encounter. Failing in this he retired behind the lines. The heavy rains the previous night had made the trenches untenable for Captain Mackaye's company. The French then took position on an eminence on the north, about sixty yards distant, and the Indians took position behind trees and in tree tops. For nine hours, during a rain storm, the assailants poured an incessant shower of balls upon the little band crowded within the lines of the fort. The English replied with vigour, and toward six o clock in the evening the conflict grew in animation, and continued until eight o clock. Washington's tranquil presence encouraged his men and deceived the enemy.

Road Over Which Washington's Men Pulled the Cannon by Hand

Washington Makes His First and His Last Surrender

De Villiers, fearing his ammunition would fail, proposed a parley, which Washington at first declined, but when repeated it was granted. The articles of capitulation were written in the French language, which, after sundry modifications in Washington's favour, were signed in duplicate in the rain, by the light of a candle by Captain James Mackaye, Lieutenant Colonel George Washington and Coulon Villiers. According to the articles agreed to, the garrison were allowed to remove all their belongings except the artillery and to march out with drums beating, and to have protection from insult or injury by the French or Indians. The English were to deliver up the officers, two cadets and the prisoners made at the defeat of Jumonville, and send them under safeguard to Fort Duquesne within two months and a half at the farthest. A duplicate of the articles was fixed upon one of the posts of the stockade. Jacob Van Braam and Robert Stobo, both captains, were delivered as hostages to the French officer as surety for the faithful compliance of the English to the articles of capitulation.

There were at the encampment at the Great Meadows at the time of the surrender about four hundred persons.

In this engagement it is reported that Washington lost thirty men killed and forty-two wounded. Captain Mackaye's loss was never reported. The French had two men killed and seventy wounded, two whereof were Indians.

By daylight the following morning the English flag was struck and the French flag took its place. The humiliated garrison took the situation as cheerfully as possible under the circumstances, and with banners flying and drums beating, the little army wended its way towards Will's Creek. In its wake followed a retinue of settlers and adherents. The lilies of France now floated in undisputed victory over every fort, trading post and mission from the Allegheny Mountains westward to the Mississippi River. No sooner had the English garrison filed out of Fort Necessity than the French began its demolition. This accomplished to their gratification they began retracing their steps toward the mouth of Redstone the same day, for fear of re-enforcements as had been requested by Washington, and encamped about two leagues distant—perhaps at the Big Rock, where the Half-King had encamped the night before the attack on Jumonville. Doubtless De Villiers turned aside and visited the spot where his half-brother had fallen and tenderly covered the remains with earth and stone to prevent their destruction by wild beasts and to mark the spot of their last resting place.

They reached the abandoned entrenchment at Grist's on the fifth, and after demolishing what was of it they burned all the contiguous houses. They reached the mouth of Redstone at ten o'clock next day, where they proceeded to burn the Hangard and then re-embarked on the Monongahela, returning to Fort Duquesne on the seventh.

Fort Necessity was in a glade between two eminences, which were covered with forests, except within sixty yards of it. The road by which Washington's army had advanced passed within a few feet on the south, and Great Meadow run skirted the base line on the north.

The fort was in the form of an obtuse angled triangle of one hundred and five degrees, its base resting on Great Meadow Run, about two perches of which were thrown across the stream and connected with the base by lines perpendicular to the opposite lines of the triangle. The base was eleven perches long, the western seven perches and the eastern line six perches. About fifty square perches of land, or nearly one-third of an acre, were included within these lines. The embankments in 1816 were still three feet high above the level of the meadow. The outside trenches, in which Captain Mackaye's men were stationed when the fight began, and from which they were flooded out, were already filled up, but inside the lines were ditches of about two feet in depth, formed by throwing the earth up against the palisades. It is ten miles east of Uniontown, and about eight hundred yards south of the National Road.

The swivel cannon captured at the surrender, excepting the one allowed to be taken away by Washington's men, were left at the fort, where in after years they were found and used by emigrants for firing salutes. Eventually they were taken to Kentucky to be used by the settlers in defence against the Indians.

The night following the surrender Washington's army encamped barely three miles distant from the fort. It laboriously wended its way, the sick and wounded being carried by their fellows, to Wills Creek, where the foremost arrived on the ninth.

Personnel of the Officers Engaged

M. Coulon de Villiers, captain of His Majesty's troops, was a half-brother to Jumonville, and was of a family of seven brothers, six of whom lost their lives in the American wars. De Villiers was taken prisoner by the English at the capture of Fort Niagara in 1770.

Captain Mackaye assisted Colonel James Innes in the construction of Fort Cumberland, and afterward became one of the justices of the peace for Westmoreland County, Pa., and lived at Pittsburgh. He had been holding court at Hannastown and returned home on the ninth of April, 1774, and was arrested on the following day by Dr. Connelly under authority of the governor of Virginia. Connelly was holding court at Fort Dunmore under authority of Virginia, and Mackaye holding court at Hannastown under authority of Pennsylvania. He was sent, with other justices, to Staunton to be lodged in jail, but was permitted to go to Williamsburg, to present an account of his arrest and was allowed to return home. Colonel Mackaye was stationed at Kittanning to succeed Van Swearingen at Fort Armstrong in July 20, 1776, with his battalion, and remained at that post until the fifteenth of December, when he was, against the remonstrances of the inhabitants, ordered elsewhere.

Captain Adam Stephens, to whom Washington gave a major's commission, became a captain in the Virginia regiment at Braddock's defeat and was wounded in the action at that time. He rose to be a colonel in the Virginia troops, and was with Grant at his defeat at Fort Duquesne. He became a brigadier general, and in February, 1779, was made a major general in the Revolutionary War. He was stationed at Fort Cumberland in November 1775, as lieutenant colonel by Governor Innes, of North Carolina, who had been in command at that place. While here there arose a dispute between Stephens and Captain Dagworthy as to rank, and Major General Shirley, who had succeeded Braddock in command of the colonies, had Dagworthy removed.

General Stephens was born about 1718 in Pennsylvania., and migrated to Virginia in 1738. He died in 1791 and was buried on his own plantation, a part of which is now embraced within the town limits of Martinsburg, Virginia.

Captain Robert Stobo was the only son of William Stobo, a merchant of Glasgow, in which city Robert was born in 1727. His father and mother both dying when he was young, he came to Virginia to serve in a store which was owned by some Glasgow merchants. He became a favourite of Governor Dinwiddie, who in 1754 appointed him the oldest captain of the Virginia regiment then raised. He was the engineer of Fort Necessity, and was one of the two hostages given up by Washington to be taken by the French to Fort Duquesne to be there held until the return of the French officers taken in the fight with Jumonville. The governor of Virginia refusing to comply with Washington's agreement and release the French officers, Stobo with Van Braam was sent to Canada.

They were the first English military prisoners at Fort Duquesne. He was allowed much privilege as a prisoner until after the defeat of Braddock, when a great change was made in the treatment he received. The plans of Fort Duquesne, an exact description of which he had forwarded to Governor Dinwiddie, and the information he had furnished, were captured among Braddock's effects and published. The consequence was that Stobo was ordered into close confinement. Subsequently he was tried and sentenced to be executed. The sentence was deferred, and at length he effected his escape and arrived at Louisburg, on the Island of Cape Breton, shortly after General Wolf had sailed for Quebec. He immediately returned to Quebec and afforded General Wolf much important information. He returned to Virginia in 1759, from whence he went to England. His heirs got an extra allowance of one thousand pounds and nine thousand acres of land in Kentucky for his services.

Captain Jacob Van Braam, as well as Adjutant Muse, had been a campaigning comrade of Lawrence Washington, and had been in the British army. He professed to be a complete master of fencing, and gave George Washington, when a youth, instructions in sword exercise. He was a Dutchman who knew a little French, and having served Washington as a French interpreter the previous year on his mission to the forts on French creek, he was called upon to interpret the articles of capitulation at the surrender of Fort Necessity. It was through his stupidity as an interpreter that Washington was placed under the ban of an assassin by the French.

For this blunder Van Braam was condemned of treachery by the House of Burgesses. He was given up by Washington to the French to be held as a hostage, along with Captain Stobo, until the return of the French officers taken at the defeat of Jumonville. By the refusal of Governor Dinwiddie to comply with Washington's agreement Van Braam was kept some time at Fort Duquesne and then sent to Quebec, along with Captain Stobo, where he was held until the conquest of Canada by the English. He returned to Virginia in 1760. He was awarded an allowance of five hundred pounds and nine thousand acres of land in Kentucky for his services.

Captain Andrew Lewis became a captain in Braddock's campaign, but had no command in the fatal action. He was with Major Grant in his defeat at Grant's Hill in 1758. He became the General Lewis of Bottetourt in the great battle with the Indians at Point Pleasant in Dunmore's war of 1774, and was a distinguished general officer in the Revolution. It was he whom it was said Washington recommended for commander-in-chief of the American army.

Lieutenant William Polson became a captain in Braddock's

campaign and was killed in the defeat. He was a native of Scotland.

Ensign Peyronie was a French Protestant chevalier, settled in Virginia, was badly wounded in the attack on Fort Necessity and became a Virginia captain in Braddock's campaign. He was killed on the field.

Dr. James Craik, a Scotchman by birth, but a resident of Alexandria, Virginia, had long been a friend and the family physician of Washington. He accompanied Washington as physician and surgeon from the beginning to the end of this campaign. He attended Colonel Fry, who died at Will's Creek from injuries sustained by the falling of his horse. He was the companion of Washington when on his journey to the west in 1770, and was also his physician through his last illness. He entered the Revolutionary army as a surgeon and rose to the first rank. He was director-in-chief of the military hospital at Yorktown in 1781. He named one of his sons George Washington Craik. who became private secretary to President Washington in his second term. Dr. Craik was willed a chair and a desk, as mementoes, by Washington.

Besides drawing his pay as both officer and surgeon in the campaign of 1754, Dr. Craik was awarded one thousand seven hundred and ninety-four acres of land. On the third of September, 1788, he obtained from Pennsylvania patents for two tracts of land in Franklin township, Fayette county, Pennsylvania. One was known as "Bowland's Camp", and the other as "Freeman Sword", each containing four hundred and three acres. They were both sold the twenty-seventh of March, 1791, to Samuel Bryson. Dr. Craik died on his plantation, within five miles of Mt. Vernon, on the sixth of February, 1814.

Queen Aliquippa, with her son, lived at the confluence of the Youghiogheny with the Monongahela. She was an Indian squaw of some importance among her people, and received her royal title from the English. She became offended because Washington did not stop to see her on his way to the French forts in November, 1753, an offence for which he fully atoned on his return by presenting her with a few presents, among which the most highly prized was a bottle of rum.

Christopher Gist was of English descent. his grandfather, Christopher Gist, died in Baltimore county in 1691. His father, Richard Gist, was a surveyor; was one of the commissioners in 1729 for laying off the town of Baltimore, and was presiding magistrate in 1736. Christopher was one of three sons—Christopher, Thomas and Nathaniel, who all married sisters. Christopher had three sons—Nathaniel, Richard, Thomas—and two daughters, Nancy and Violet. He was a leading character of the times, being by nature an adventurer.

In 1748 his residence was on the Yadkin, in North Carolina. He was employed by the "Ohio Company" in locating their grant of five hundred thousand acres of land on the Ohio River, the duties of which he performed in the years 1751 and 1752. On his return to his home in the former year he found the Indians had made an incursion into that settlement, had murdered many of his neighbours and burned the houses. His family had fled to the banks of the Roanoke, in Virginia, a distance of thirty-five miles. His residence was on the Yadkin River, and on the west side of a stream known as Sawmill Creek, near and west of Reddie's River, near the present town of Wilkesbarre, in Wilkes County, .North Carolina. He was residing at Wills Creek when Washington secured his services as guide to the French posts, near Lake Erie, in November, 1753. On their way out and also on their return he stopped at Gist's new settlement at the western foot of Laurel Hill. Washington also spent the night with Gist at Will's Creek on his return.

With his sons, Nathaniel and Thomas, he was with Braddock on the fatal field, and for his services received a grant of twelve thousand acres of land from the king of England. He, with George Croghan, assisted in building the stockade at the Forks of the Ohio for the Ohio Company in 1754, and was purchasing agent for the Virginia soldiers stationed at Fort Mount Pleasant. After the defeat of Braddock, 1755 till 1765, he was engaged in various public capacities in the south and south-west. In the latter year he returned to his settlement west of the mountains, and after settling his family, he returned to his old home where he died of smallpox.

His son, Thomas Gist, remained at this new settlement until his death, in 1786, and was a man of considerable influence. Richard was killed at the battle of King's Mountain. Nancy made her home with Thomas until his death, when she moved with her brother Nathaniel to their grant in Kentucky, where the family of Nathaniel Gist became quite prominent. Violet married William Cromwell, and lived on this new settlement.

What at that time was known as the Gist Plantation was subsequently warranted by Virginia to Thomas Gist in right of Christopher Gist. There were five surveys made the twenty-sixth of October, 1785, aggregating two thousand, five hundred acres in one body. After the death of Thomas Gist this whole tract was sold to Colonel Isaac Meason, who gave it the name of Mt. Braddock. On this he erected a large stone mansion in 1802. His son, Isaac Meason, Jr., succeeded him in the possession of this farm, and after the death of the latter his widow sold it to Isaac Beeson.

Dr. Hugh Mercer was a Scotchman, having fled to Virginia from the service of the Pretender, on the fatal field of Culloden. He accompanied the Virginia troops as a surgeon. He also accompanied Braddock's army and was badly wounded on the fatal field. Being unable to escape in the general flight, he concealed himself behind a tree, from which place he was a forced witness to the scalping and plundering of the dead and dying. After darkness he left his hiding place and by the aid of the stars and streams, after several days of painful suffering, reached Fort Cumberland. He served as captain in Colonel Armstrong's expedition against the Indians at Kittanning, in 1756, from which he again returned severely wounded to Fort Cumberland. He finally became a field officer in the Revolution and fell at Princeton in January, 1777.

The Proprietaries of Pennsylvania, on March 2, 1771, granted to Dr. Hugh Mercer, of Fredericksburg, Virginia, two tracts of land, about three and a half miles from Stewart's Crossing, now in Bullskin township, Fayette County, containing two hundred and eighty-two and one-half, and three hundred and eleven acres respectively, and the usual allowance. These tracts were sold by the executors of Dr. Mercer to Isaac Meason the third of November, 1789.

Lieutenant Thomas Waggener, with his company, supported that of Washington at the attack on Jumonville, and these two companies received all the fire of the enemy. In this action he was wounded. He subsequently became a captain of the Virginia troops and as such accompanied Braddock in his campaign and displayed in that fatal action signal good sense and gallantry, and escaped unhurt.

Tanacharison was a Seneca chief of great note, being head *sachem* of the mixed tribes which had migrated to the Ohio and its tributaries. He was surnamed the Half-King, being subordinate to the Iroquois confederacy. Washington pronounced him a man of more than usual intelligence. In the spring of 1753, the Miami tribes under the leadership of Half-King, made a treaty at Carlisle with Benjamin Franklin, at which they plighted their friendship to the English. That Half-King proved faithful to his vow, history offers ample proof. His home was at Logstown, whence he accompanied Washington to the French forts in 1753. He was at the Forks of the Ohio when Ensign Ward surrendered that post, and vehemently protested against the conduct of the French commander on that occasion. He rendered invaluable service in the detection and defeat of Jumonville, and by his discretion and unswerving loyalty had won the admiration of Washington.

When Washington's little army retraced its steps over the mountains, Half-King took his family and went to Aughwick, in Pennsylvania, where they were maintained at the expense of the colony. A short time after his removal to Aughquick he was taken sick and in October of this same year he died. His death was mourned with great lamentation by both the Indians and the whites. Scarooyada succeeded him as sachem of the Delaware tribe. In April, 1755, the colony of Pennsylvania refused longer to support them and their destitute families. This treatment and that received at the hands of Braddock, created an antipathy in the breasts of the hitherto friendly Indians.

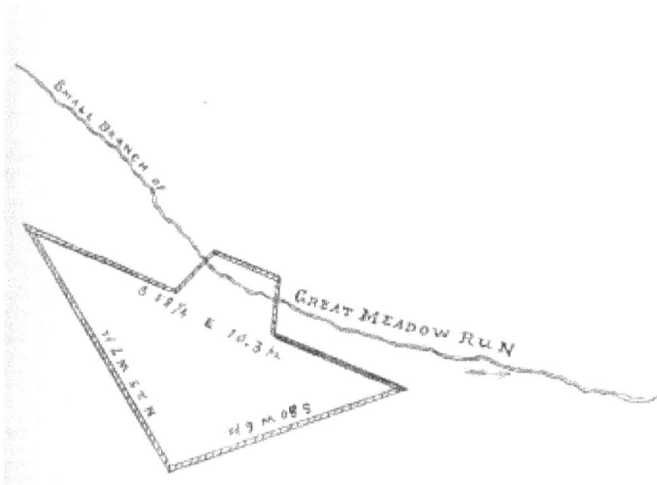

FORT NECESSITY AS SKETCHED BY FREEMAN LEWIS - 1816

Washington Retires to Mt. Vernon

In 1752 the Ohio Company concluded to establish this as a permanent trading-post, although this point was eighty miles west of the frontier settlements. Here they erected another storehouse and magazine, which was known as the New Storehouse. This was located on the Virginia side of the Potomac, and was near the place now occupied by the abutment of the Potomac bridge. This structure was built of logs and was sufficiently commodious to accommodate a garrison and afford protection to settlers in case of an attack by Indians.

Washington proceeded to Williamsburg, where he made a full report of the campaign to Governor Dinwiddie, and after receiving a vote of thanks from the House of Burgesses for his bravery and gallant defence of his country, he retired to his home at Mount Vernon.

After Washington's return to Williamsburg Colonel James Innes, a Scotchman by birth, but a resident of North Carolina, marched to Wills Creek and on the first of September, 1754, took command of that post, which had been garrisoned by Rutherford's and Clark's independent companies from New York. These had been sent to join Washington, but got no farther than Winchester.

Colonel Innes constructed a fort at the mouth of Will's Creek, with the assistance of Captain Mackaye, beginning the twelfth of September and completing the work in about one month. This he named Fort Mount Pleasant. It was garrisoned during the winter of 1754-55. The fort proper occupied almost the identical spot on which now stands the residence of James A. Milholland, known as the "Hoge House." This fort mounted four ten-pounders, besides swivels, and was favourably situated to keep the hostile Indians in check.

Washington Acquires a Title to the Site of Fort Necessity and Which He Held at the Time of His Death

As early as 1767 Washington acquired from Virginia a preemption to a tract of land of three hundred and thirty-four acres under the name of Mt. Washington, which included the site of Fort Necessity. June 13, l769, an application was sent in to the land office in right of William Brooks for three hundred acres called "Great Meadows," including an improvement made by a grant from Captain Charles Edmundstone, patented February 18, 1782, to General George Washington. The patent from the supreme Executive Council of Pennsylvania to General Washington recites that said tract of land was surveyed by virtue of an order issued June 13, 1769, by William Brooks, who by deed dated the seventeenth day of October, 1771, conveyed said tract of land and the appurtenances unto George Washington in fee simple, and a warrant of acceptance of the survey issued to him, dated February 14, 1782. The consideration paid by Washington to the commonwealth of Pennsylvania was thirty-three pounds, fifteen shillings and eight pence, Pennsylvania money, which was some less than one hundred dollars.

This tract was referred to in his last will, and owned by him at the time of his death.

In December, 1776, the Virginia legislature proposed as adjustment to the boundary controversy that the western line of

Maryland should be extended northward to the fortieth degree of latitude and thence westward along that parallel "until the distance of five degrees of longitude from the Delaware should be accomplished." This would have thrown the site of Fort Necessity a distance of several miles within the territory of Virginia, but no formal action was taken on the part of Pennsylvania to this proposition. The running of the Mason and Dixon line put an end to all controversy and secured to the Keystone state one of her cherished historic sites.

After the death of Washington his executors sold it to Andrew Parks, of Baltimore, whose wife, Harriet, was a relative and legatee of Washington. She sold it to General Thomas Meason, who sold it to Joseph Huston, from whom it was sold to Colonel Samuel Evans for the taxes in 1824, and (it seems to have reverted back to Huston) sold as property of Huston by the sheriff to Honourable Nathaniel Ewing, who sold it to James Sampey, April 6, 1836, whose executors sold it to Godfrey Fazenbaker, December 29, 1856, for four thousand dollars. Mr. Fazenbaker's deed contained the following clause:

> Excepting and reserving that piece heretofore conveyed by said executors to the Fort Necessity Washington Monument Association, with right of way and privileges, but if the conditions of the said association are not complied with the reservation is a nullity.

Mr. Fazenbaker, however, agreed to extend the time almost indefinitely should the association continue its efforts to erect a monument at the old stockade.

Mr. Lewis Fazenbaker, the son of Godfrey Fazenbaker, is the present owner of the farm and says that the site of the fort has never been, nor never shall be, plowed over while it remains in the Fazenbaker name.

Washington owned at the time of his death over sixteen hundred acres of land in Franklin and Washington townships, on which was erected a flouring mill, which is still in operation. This tract of land was sold to Colonel Israel Shreeve.

An act of assembly was passed April 6, 1850, incorporating the Fort Necessity Washington Monument Association, making Daniel Sturgeon, John Washington, Samuel Y. Campbell, John Huston, Hervey Morris, Robert P. Flenniken, Andrew Stewart, Sebastian Rush, Daniel Kaine, Joshua B. Howell, William Stone, Zalmon Ludington and Isaac Beeson, of Fayette County, and "all other persons who have subscribed, or shall hereafter subscribe, any sum for the erection of a monument under the provisions of this act, and their successors or assigns, be and are hereby made a body corporate under the style of Fort Necessity Washington Monument Association, the property of this corporation to be forever exempt from taxation.

The first election of officers was to be held the first Monday in May, 1850, and thereafter to be held on the twenty-second day of February each year. The board of managers held their first meeting at the house of Samuel Y. Campbell, May 6, 1850, but for lack of a quorum, agreed to meet at the office of R. P. Flenniken, Esq., Saturday, the eleventh. At this meeting Samuel Y. Campbell was elected president; Andrew Stewart, Hervey Morris, Joshua B. Howell, Samuel A. Gilmore and R. P. Flenniken, managers, and Isaac Beeson, treasurer.

A committee, consisting of Andrew Stewart, Sebastian Rush, Samuel Y. Campbell and Thomas R. Davidson, was appointed to secure a title to one acre of ground, embracing the site of Fort Necessity, together with right of way thereto. Two agents were appointed in each township of the county to solicit subscriptions for the purchase of the ground and the erection of the monument. At a meeting of the managers, June twenty-second, Mr. Stewart presented the form of a deed of conveyance from the executors of James Sampey, conveying to the corporation one acre of ground, including the site of the fort, which form it was agreed should be executed.

Requests for contributions were sent to the President of the United States, the different heads of departments, the representatives m Congress from Pennsylvania, Maryland, Virginia and South Carolina, the literary institutions of the state, the governor, and to Major Delafield and cadets of West Point, the Masonic and Odd Fellow lodges and encampments of the state.

An effort was made March 2, 1852, to have the Topographical Department at Washington appoint a gentleman of the department to visit the site of Fort Necessity and make a drawing, as near as circumstances would permit, of the original stockade for the purpose of having the same lithographed, to be used as an inducement for subscriptions.

On August 6, 1851, Captain F. Clarke, who was then at Brownsville, was written to and solicited to visit the site and make a draft of the location and environs. On August 14, 1851, Captain K. Dawson was also requested to make a draft of the same.

Agents were sent out to canvass Fayette and neighbouring counties for subscriptions. Some little money was obtained; some of the solicitors proved to be defaulters, and what funds did find their way to the treasury were consumed in stationery, postage and clerical work. So, after several months of heroic effort in a noble cause the Fort Necessity Washington Monument Association was doomed to a lingering death.

In 1854, J. N. H. Patrick, Esq., editor of the Democratic Sentinel of Uniontown, Pa,, urged a celebration to be held on the Fourth day of July of that year with a view of making a move toward the erection of a monument at the site of the old stockade. Lodge No. 228 A.Y. M. of Uniontown and a large concourse of citizens visited the place and conducted suitable ceremonies, and a corner stone was placed near the centre of the enclosure. David Shriver Stewart son of Hon. Andrew Stewart, performed the last named ceremony.

Not long after the corner-stone was laid the contents, whatever they may have been, were removed, and some six years ago, the upper stone was pried from its position, broken in two and left on the surface of the ground, a sad reminder of the vandalism liable to be perpetrated on any sacred object. The embankments have been worn down m the lapse of years until they are scarcely larger than a furrow thrown up with a plow yet much of the outlines can be easily traced.

WASHINGTON'S MILL, BUILT IN FAYETTE COUNTY - 1776

In January, 1899, Hon. T. Robb Deyarmon, of Fayette County, introduced in the lower House a bill entitled, "An act providing for the acquisition by the state of certain grounds at Fort Necessity, Fayette County, and making an appropriation of ten thousand dollars therefore." This bill got as far as the committee on appropriations, and there it was buried in oblivion.

A magnificent and patriotic celebration was held on the site of Fort Necessity, July 4th, 1904, in commemoration of the one hundred and fiftieth anniversary of the surrender of that fort.

The patriotic sentiment of the citizens of Fayette County was aroused when Fort Necessity Lodge of I. O. O. F. took the initiative in a celebration of the one hundred and fiftieth anniversary of the surrender of Fort Necessity. Pressing invitations were sent throughout Fayette and adjoining counties, urging mat an enthusiastic meeting be held at the site of the old fort and that patriotic addresses appropriate to the occasion be made.

The suggestion met with a most happy response, and upon the day of the occasion, long before daylight, the roads leading to this historic spot were crowded with vehicles and persons on foot.

A grand parade was formed on the National Road under Chief Marshal Lieutenant Colonel Everhart Bierer and his *aide*, M. A. Keifer, followed by Rutter's Silver Cornet Band, Co. C of Uniontown under command of Captain A. G. Beeson, Co. D of Connellsville under command of Captain John L. Gans, Uniontown Fire Department, Co. A Boys Brigade under Lieutenant Chas. Hall, Co. E under Sergeant-Major L. S. Sloan, Co. F under First Sergeant Jay W. Johns, Co. G under First Lieutenant Ralph C. Kennedy and all under the command of Adjutant I. E. .Keener.

Next came the Soldiers orphans from the Jumonville Soldiers' Orphan school under the care of Superintendent John A. Waters, Fort Necessity Lodge I. O. O. F., followed by a cavalcade most imposing.

It is estimated that fully 8,000 people participated m the celebration of the occasion, and it can be truthfully stated that not the slightest disorder marred the enjoyment of the day.

The officers of this celebration committee were, President, Hon. E. H. Reppert, Secretary, James Hadden, Treasurer, M. H. Bowman. These were ably assisted by not only many of the prominent citizens of the town but throughout the county.

The meeting at the grove was presided over by Hon. E. H. Reppert who introduced the speakers. Rev. F. E. J. Lloyd of the Episcopal Church pronounced the invocation, after which Judge Reppert made some happy introductory remarks and then introduced Robert F. Hopwood who read the Declaration of Independence. Hon. George C. Sturgis of Morgantown, West Virginia delivered a most able and patriotic address. He was followed by Rev. Father A. A. Lambing of Wilkinsburg. The next speaker was Judge F. G. White of Pontiac, Ill.

Letters of regret from Senator P. C Knox, Hon. Hampton L. Carson, Hon. J. P. Dolliver, Hon. Lott Thomas, John W. Beazell, Hon. Boyd Crumrine, Dr. T. N. Boyle, Dr. C. W. Smith, Dr. Camden M. Coburn and General M. I. Ludington were read by John S. Ritenour, and the benediction was pronounced by Rev. W. H. Gladden of the M. P. Church of Connellsville.

The services at the grove were enjoyed to the utmost by the vast throng who gave the speakers most respectful attention.

A most bountiful dinner was served in the grove, after which a sham-battle took place between the troops, and another between the members of the boys' brigade all of which were greatly enjoyed by the spectators.

The site of Fort Necessity remained unmarked until July 4th, 1908, when a tablet was erected thereon bearing the following inscription:

This tablet marks the site

of

Fort Necessity

where Lieutenant Colonel George Washington, in command of four hundred provincial troops, after an engagement of nine hours, capitulated to M. Coulon de Villiers, in command of nine hundred French regulars and their

Indian allies, on July 4th 1754.

Washington lost thirty men killed and forty-two wounded. Captain Mackaye's loss was never reported. The French had two men killed and seventy wounded, two whereof were Indians.

Erected July 4th, 1908, under the auspices of the Centennial Celebration committee of 1904.

General Edward Braddock

Expedition of Major General Edward Braddock Against the French at Fort Duquesne, 1755

Edward Braddock was born in Perthshire, Scotland, about 1695, and was the only son of Major General Braddock. He entered the army as ensign in the Grenadier company, second regiment of the Coldstream Guards, on the eleventh of October, 1710, at the age of fifteen years. This was a very aristocratic division of the British army, and the bodyguard of royalty. From this his promotions were rapid.

On the twenty-fifth of November, 1754, Major General Edward Braddock was commissioned general-in-chief of His Majesty's forces in North America and received his instructions concerning his duties in relation to the encroachments of the French. Becoming impatient of the preparation of the troops he set sail from Cork aboard the *Norwich* on the twenty-first of December, 1754, and arrived at Alexandria, Virginia, February 20, 1755. His troops—the Forty-Fourth Regiment, under Colonel Sir Peter Halket, and the Forty-Eighth Regiment, under Colonel Dunbar—set sail on the fourteenth of January and landed in March, 1755, and marched to Alexandria. These regiments were of the royal troops, and numbered five hundred men each.

A council was held at Alexandria on the fourteenth of April, at which were present Honourable Augustus Keppel, commander-in-chief of His Majesty's ships, and the governors of Massachusetts, Virginia, New York, Pennsylvania and Maryland. Here three expeditions were planned, one of which was to be under the command of General Braddock with the British troops, with such aid as might be derived from Maryland and Virginia, to which were afterward added two independent companies from New York.

General Braddock was to move against the French at Fort Duquesne, and from thence to Canada. With this object in view he marched from Alexandria the twentieth of April, and reached Fredericktown, Maryland, on the twenty-fourth. Passing through Winchester he reached Fort Mount Pleasant on the ninth of May, to which point Sir John Sinclair, deputy quartermaster general, had preceded him about two weeks. General Braddock, having been designated by the Duke of Cumberland the captain general of the British army, requested of Governor Dinwiddie that the name of the new fort be changed from Fort Mount Pleasant to that of Fort Cumberland, by which name it was ever afterward known. Here, on the 10th of May, Washington was appointed *aide-de-camp* to His Excellency, Major General Braddock.

Braddock's army now consisted of the Forty-Fourth Regiment, English infantry, Colonel Sir Peter Halket; the Forty-Eighth, Colonel Thomas Dunbar; sundry independent colonial companies, a company of horse, a company of artillery, a company of marines, etc. The two independent companies of New York, under command of Captains Rutherford and Gates, the latter to whom Burgoyne surrendered at Saratoga, had garrisoned the fort during the winter of 1754-55. The field officers were Lieutenant Colonels Burton and Gage, the latter of Bunker Hill notoriety; Majors Chapman and Sparks, Major Sir John Sinclair, quartermaster general; Matthew Leslie, his assistant; Captain Robert Orme, of the Coldstream Guards; Christopher Gist and his son Nathaniel as guides; Drs. James Clark and Hugh Mercer. These had been with Washington in his campaign the previous year.

Braddock was here tendered the valuable services also of

George Croghan, the Indian agent of Aughwick; Montour, the Indian diplomatist; Monacatootha, the successor of Half-King, whose acquaintance and friendship Washington had formed when on his mission to Le Boeuf, with about 150 Seneca and Delaware Indians, and Captain Jack with his company of warriors and scouts. These offered their services without pay and to furnish their own arms, all on conditions that they were to dress, march and fight as they pleased and to be free from strict military discipline,

With such a strict disciplinarian as Braddock such conditions could not for one moment be considered and the offer was peremptorily refused, whereupon Captain Jack with his band, together with nearly every Indian, turned upon his heel in disgust and marched back to the hills of the Juniata.

Had Braddock accepted the services of these experienced warriors and scouts the result of his expedition can only now be conjectural, but the consequence of his refusal and of his strict adherence to discipline has amply recorded.

Captain Jack, who was also known as "Susquehanna Jack,", "The Black Rifle," "The Black Hunter," and "The Wild Hunter of the Juniata," was a large, powerful and fearless frontier settler of the valley of the Juniata, through whose veins ran a goodly mixture of Indian if not a baser blood.

Once upon returning from a long and weary chase he was horrified to find his cabin in ashes and the corpses of his murdered family scattered around. From this time to the day of his death his thirst for Indian blood could never be satisfied. His fame as an Indian fighter soon spread from the head springs of the Susquehanna to the Potomac.

The old pathway along which Captain Jack travelled, and in which he met his dusky foe in mortal combat, and in which so many fell a victim to his deadly rule, is still plainly visible.

His bones repose in a lonely grave near his favourite spring at the base of the mountain which bears his name and stands as a towering monument to perpetuate his memory.

Reference has frequently been made to a monument that

stands in the Falling Spring cemetery at Chambersburg, Pa., which bears the following inscription:

Colonel Patrick Jack, an officer of the Colonial and Revolutionary wars, died January 25th, 1829, aged 91 years.

This latter was not the Captain Jack who offered his services to Braddock, but was a resident of Chambersburg at the time of his death.

Monacatootha, known also as Scarooyada, with a few of his followers, not more than eight in number, however, followed Braddock through the campaign and rendered valuable service. At a council held at Onondago by the Six Nations. Monacatootha had been selected to succeed Tanacharison or Half-King, as *sachem*. The clever pencil of the artist could not throw upon canvass a more dignified specimen of the noble race. The majestic form of this warrior as it towered above his followers leading the van, followed by the glittering array of the first disciplined army whose martial tread ever awoke the echoes of these primeval forests, was grand in the extreme. His leggings were frilled with locks from the dried scalps of his conquered foes; his own scalp lock, plaited down his back, a well understood token of defiance, over which waved the plume feathers of the eagle, the emblem of American liberty, was further gaudily ornamented with the gorgeous plumage of the blue jay. On his noble breast was plainly tattooed a tomahawk, the emblem of war, and on each cheek he bore the signs of the hunter, the bow and arrow. The army had marched but a little over twenty miles from Fort Cumberland when Monacatootha, who was a little in advance, was surrounded and taken by some French and Indians. The former were determined to put him to death but the latter remonstrated and even threatened to join the English should the French carry out their design. The *sachem* was then lashed to a tree and left to his fate, but fortunately was soon found and released by his son and other Indians.

While the army was encamped at Thicketty Run, July 4th, two of Monacatootha's men were sent to reconnoitre and re-

FORT CUMBERLAND - 1755

turned with the scalp of a French officer which they had succeeded in taking within half a mile of the fort.

On July 6th, while the army was on the march from Thicketty Run, by a disregard of a pre-concerted signal, Monacatootha's son was fired upon and killed by some outrangers of Braddock's army. The general displayed great sorrow for the unfortunate occurrence and after due expressions of sympathy and donations caused the body to be buried in the honours of war at the next encampment, which also received the name of Monacatootha in honour of the bereaved *sachem*.

The Colonial Records and the Pennsylvania Archives bear ample evidence that this noble *sachem* not only held a commission under the province of Pennsylvania, but that his mature judgement was sought in the deliberations of the councils of the same.

Braddock's whole force amounted to about 2150 men at Fort Cumberland. But by haughtily rejecting the proffered services of the Indians as scouts and guides, many of them retired to the mountains of the Juniata. Scarooyada and a few others, however, followed Braddock throughout the campaign. This *sachem* afterward, in a speech at Philadelphia, denounced the French as cowards and the English as fools.

Braddock at this time had under his command several officers, both white and Indian, who were far more competent to command than he, and who, if permitted the opportunity, would doubtless have led the troops to victory.

On the 30th of May Sir John Sinclair and Major Chapman were sent forward with a detachment of 600 men to widen the road opened by Washington the previous year, to advance as far as the Little Meadows and there erect a fort and collect provisions. On the 7th of June the first division, under Sir Peter Halket, moved forward and on the 8th the second division, under Lieutenant Colonel Gage, of the Forty-Fourth, and on the 10th the main body of the army, with the commander-in-chief left Fort Cumberland.

Through the influence of Dr. Benjamin Franklin 150 wagons

and 2000 horses joined Braddock on the 8th of June, and the army was enabled to move. The first camp was called "Camp at the Grove", and from here orders were issued, and the commander-in-chief rested till the 12th. He encamped at "Martin's" on Saturday, June 14th. The army was seven days in reaching the Little Meadows, a distance of twenty miles from Fort Cumberland. Here a council was held, at which it was determined that General Braddock, with 1200 men and twelve pieces of cannon, should press on, leaving Colonel Dunbar and Major Chapman to follow by easy stages. At the Little Crossings, two miles west of the Little Meadows, Washington was taken down with a fever and was left under the care of Dr. Craik and a guard to await the arrival of Colonel Dunbar, who came up in two days. Washington had exacted, however, from Braddock, a promise not to make the attack on Fort Duquesne until he came up. The army reached the Great Crossings, a distance of seventeen miles farther west, on the 23rd.

The first encampment on Fayette County soil was at the "Twelve Springs," having marched from Squaw's Fort, near the Big Crossings, six miles. This encampment was between what is now known as Mount Augusta and Marlow's, and south of the National Road. Here the army encamped the 24th.

On the 25th the army made a memorable march. Within about a quarter of a mile after starting a bluff was reached over which it was necessary to let down the carriages by the use of ropes and tackle. During the day's march three men were killed and scalped by the enemy, and some French and Indians were fired upon by the sentinels.

The Site of Fort Necessity Passed Without Notice

The ruins of Fort Necessity were passed without halt or seeming notice, and the army camped about one mile beyond the Great Meadows after a march of seven miles. This encampment is known as the Old Orchard Camp, and was reached late in the day. There may have been some superstitions belief which caused Braddock to pass the Great Meadows without a halt.

Nothing was farther from the proud commander's mind while encamped at this place than the thought that within a little more than a fortnight the same should witness the disordered retreat of the remnant of his defeated army, should hear his dying moans and be his sepulchre, but such it proved to be.

The following day (26th) Braddock offered a bounty of five pounds for every scalp that his Indians and soldiers should take. On account of the roughness of the road the march was a distance of four miles only. This encampment was known as "Rock Fort" or "Great Rock," and was near a fine spring, now known as Washington's Spring. The rock was situated on the crest, of Laurel Mill, and near the same as occupied by Half-King the year before, when he notified Washington of the approach of Jumonville's party. Here they found another Indian camp, which had just been deserted. The fire was still burning, and a commission was found indicating that the party was under the command of Sieur Normanville.

From Rock Fort the army marched on the 27th northward

along the crest of Laurel Hill, passing within a few hundred feet of the scene of Jumonville's defeat, and to the eastward of the prominence, at the western foot of which was lately located the Jumonville Orphan school, and encamped at Gist's plantation, where Washington had commenced a stockade the year before, a distance of some eight miles from Rock port.

On the 28th the army marched to the Youghiogheny and encamped at Stewart's Crossing, a short distance below where the town of Connellsville now stands. The crossing was effected on the 30th, and the army pursued a north-easterly course and passed through where the town of Mount Pleasant now stands, and west of Greensburg to Bush fork of Turtle Creek. Here Braddock left the Nemacolin Trail and turning to the westward encamped about two miles distant from the Monongahela River. Here Washington joined him on the evening of July 8th, he having come forward with a detachment of 100 men with packhorses and provisions on July 3rd, and was hauled to this place in a covered wagon.

At 3 o'clock on the morning of July 9th Colonel Thomas Gage led the advance and crossed to the west bank of the Monongahela by 8 o'clock, with a body of 300 men. He was immediately followed by another body of 200 men. Next came the general with the column of artillery, the main body of the army and the baggage. This crossing was near the site of the present town of McKeesport. The army then marched down three miles and halted to take dinner. Washington describes the march and manoeuvres of the army at this place to be the grandest sight he had ever beheld. The recrossing was effected just below the mouth of Turtle Creek, and by 1 o'clock the whole had recrossed the river.

The Assault

Almost at this moment a sharp fire was heard upon the advance party, under Colonel Gage, who was now ascending the hill about 100 yards from the terminus of the plain. A heavy fire of musketry was poured in upon his troops by an invisible foe. The fire was returned at random, consequently to no effect.

The advance became panic stricken and fell back, the officers all the while trying in vain to cause a rally and restore order. For nearly three hours the troops huddled together in confusion in the narrow pass and were being shot down by the enemy hidden in the ravines on each side. The Virginia provincials, understanding the Indian mode of warfare, would have taken to the trees and routed the enemy had Braddock permitted. He denounced them as cowards and dastards for treeing, and even struck many of them down with his sword, an act for which he soon paid the penalty, as the sequel will show.

In the confusion of the battle more than half of the whole army were either killed or wounded, two-thirds of them being shot down by their own men. Braddock had four horses killed under him and at last, while on the fifth, he received a mortal wound which shattered his right arm and penetrated his lungs. He was carried from the field. Had it not been for the devotedness of his *aide*, Captain Orme, and the fidelity of Captain Stewart, of Virginia, who was in command of the light horse, the fallen general would have had his wish gratified, that the scene of his disaster would also witness his death. He was wrapped in a silken sash taken from about his waist, which English officers were wont to carry, and was carried off the held by his faithful body servant, Bishop, whom, in his dying moments, he bequeathed to Washington.

The silken sash in which he was borne from the field was kept, and after the Mexican war was presented to General Zachary Taylor from whom it descended to his daughter, Mrs. Betty Dandridge, in whose possession it remained until her death.

BRADDOCK'S BATTLEFIELD

The Deadly Result

Out of eighty-nine commissioned officers twenty-six were killed and thirty-seven wounded, and of the soldiers 430 were killed and about 400 wounded, the killed being in excess of the wounded. Every field officer, and everyone on horseback, except Washington, who had two horses killed under him and four bullets through his coat, was either killed or carried off the held wounded. Washington that day rode upon a pillow, so enfeebled and emaciated was he from the attack of fever; and yet, with great coolness, at the head of the provincials, he formed and covered the retreat.

Sir Peter Halket and the gallant young secretary, Shirley, were among the killed. Captain Orme saved his journal, which is now so highly prized as being an authentic and continuous record of this unfortunate campaign. All the artillery, ammunition, baggage and stores, together with the dead and the dying were left on the fatal held. All the secretary's papers, with all the commanding general's orders, instructions and correspondence, together with the military chest, containing twenty-five thousand pounds in money, fell into the hands of the French. The Pennsylvania Wagoner's escaped to a man on their fleetest horses, some arriving at Dunbar's camp, a distance of forty miles, by 10 o'clock the next morning, and one or two wounded officers were carried into camp before noon of this same day.

The French Contingent

M. de Contrecoeur was in chief command at Fort Duquesne, under who were De Beaujeu and Charles de Langdale. De Beaujeu, at the head of a force of 250 French and 650 Indians, marched out of Fort Duquesne at 9 o'clock on the morning of July 9th, and by half past twelve o'clock found himself in the presence of the English. De Beaujeu fell early in the battle and soon expired, and Dumas being next in command, led the attack after De Beaujeu fell. The loss of the French was slight, but fell chiefly on the officers, three of whom were killed and four wounded. Of the regular soldiers all but four escaped unwounded. The Canadians suffered still less in proportion to their number. The Indians, who won the victory, bore the principal loss.

The remnant of Braddock's defeated army attempted to make a rally on the west side of the river to await reinforcements from Colonel Dunbar, but in this they utterly failed. The Indians made no attempt to pursue the retreating army, but contented themselves with scalping and pillaging the dead. From this place Washington was ordered on to Dunbar for wagons, provisions and hospital stores. He rode all night in the ram and darkness and reached Dunbar at daybreak.

Braddock was borne on a litter and reached Gist's plantation by 10 o'clock the next evening and lay at the Indian's spring that night awaiting surgical aid from Dunbar. Early in the night succeeding the battle many reached the deserted settlement of Gist.

Here they met wagons and provisions with Washington and a detachment of soldiers from Dunbar. These Braddock ordered to proceed to the relief of the stragglers still left behind.

Sir John Sinclair was borne into Dunbar's camp on the 10th, on a sheet, and Braddock was moved up the following day. Colonel Dunbar, with Major Chapman, had been left at the Little Meadows, to follow on by easy stages with the heavy ordnance and supplies. They passed Fort Necessity on the 2nd of July, and formed his final encampment on the summit of Laurel Hill, a flat piece of land in close proximity to a fine spring, and within a few hundred yards of the fatal action with Jumonville.

The panic-stricken fugitives came pouring into the encampment of Dunbar; the drums beat to arms, the fright became contagious, and disorder reigned supreme. By order of Braddock barrels of powder, amounting to 50,000 pounds, were staved and the contents thrown into a pool which had formed below the spring; the shells were bursted and about 150 wagons were burned to prevent them falling into the hands of the enemy. Colonel Dunbar, in his report to Governor Shirley, states positively that there was not a gun of any kind buried. Many bayonets and pieces of shells have been gathered up from the camp, and scarcely a museum of the state but contains many specimens. One collector has in his possession the half of a forty-pound shell which was made for an eight-inch gun, and two solid shot weighing twelve pounds each. These bear the English mark of the "Broad Arrow."

Since the removal of the Soldiers' Orphan school to the immediate neighbourhood of the camp, in 1875, there have been collected enough pieces of shell and balls from which two small cannons were moulded. These weigh about 200 pounds each. One is in Pittsburgh and the other is mounted and kept at the school, where it is used for firing salutes. One of these small cannons was presented to the Abe Patterson Post No. 88 G. A. R., of Allegheny City. It was mounted on lumber taken from Perry's fleet.

The retreat from Dunbar's camp was begun on the 13th, and

by the same route as the advance had been made. An encampment was made at the Old Orchard, the same place as Braddock had encamped on his way out. Braddock was silent all the first day after the defeat, and at night only said: "Who would have thought it?" All the next day he was again silent, till at last he muttered: "We shall know better how to deal with them the next time," and died in a few minutes after. Before breathing his last the dying general bequeathed his favourite charger and his body servant, Bishop, to Washington in recognition of his faithfulness as a staff officer.

Dunbar's Encampment

General Braddock's Death and Burial

General Braddock died on Sunday evening about 8 o'clock. July 13, 1755. He was wrapped in his cloak as a winding sheet and buried at daybreak on Monday morning, at the camp, in the middle of the road, that the army in passing over the grave might obliterate every trace of its whereabouts, and thus avoid any desecration of the body by the Indians. The chaplain having been wounded, Washington read the Episcopal funeral service, and the dead general was buried with the honours of war. A few days after the retreat of Dunbar the French sent out a party who advanced as far as the deserted camp, and proceeded to complete the destruction of everything destructible that could be found.

Braddock's Slayer

It has always been related that one Thomas Fausett fired the fatal shot that caused the death of General Braddock. Fausett was a soldier in Captain Cholmondeley's company, having enlisted at Shippensburg, Pa. He was a large man, of great strength, rude habits and strong passions. He had a brother Joseph who was also in the same company. In the engagement at Braddock's field the provincials took to the trees, in Indian fashion, and were doing good execution, but Braddock cursed them as dastards and cowards and cut many of them down with his sword. Tom Fausett saw the reckless general cut his brother down, and this was more than a man of his temperament could endure. He sought and obtained revenge. Fausett took up a tract of 100 acres of land at the junction of Braddock's and Dunlap's roads on the summit of Laurel Hill.

This included the site of Rock Fort or Big Rock and Washington Springs. Here he kept a tavern for several years. He sold his rights to this tract April 29, 1788, to Isaac Phillips for the sum of fifty pounds. This stand was afterward known as Slack's tavern, and was considered a good stand until the National Road was opened over the mountains. In October, 1816, Fausett was a pauper at Thomas Mitchell's, in Wharton township, and claimed then to be 104 years of age. He made his final home with Thomas Stewart, not far distant from Ohio Pyle, and at whose home he died at the remarkable age of 109, years. When intoxicated he would often relate the scenes of Braddock's defeat, and in obscure language hint to the circumstances of firing the fatal shot. He was said to have been married three times, and that two of his wives were killed by the Indians, and that his favourite, as he termed his "little Dutch wife," was tomahawked before his eyes. He died about 1820.

The Continued Retreat

The retreating army encamped at Little Meadows the following night after Braddock's death, a distance of thirty-two miles from Old Orchard Camp. Colonel Dunbar arrived at Fort Cumberland by the 18th of July, and remained there until the 2nd of August. While here he was met with earnest requests from the governors of Pennsylvania, Maryland and Virginia that he would post his troops on the frontier so as to afford some protection to the inhabitants. To all these entreaties Dunbar turned a deaf ear, and continued his hasty march through the country, not considering himself safe until he arrived at Philadelphia.

The Scattered Army

Washington remained at Fort Cumberland for a few days, being in feeble health and still suffering from the effects of his illness. While here he wrote the following letter to Governor Dinwiddie:

Fort Cumberland, July 18, 1755.

Honourable Sir:—

As I am favoured with an opportunity, I should think myself inexcusable were I to omit giving you some account of our late action with the French on the Monongahela, the 9th instant. We conducted our march from Fort Cumberland to Frazer's, which is about seven miles from Fort Duquesne, without meeting any extraordinary event, having only a straggler or two picked up by the French Indians. When we came to this place we were attacked (very unexpectedly I must own) by about 300 French and Indians. Our number consisted of about 1300 chosen men, well armed, chiefly regulars who were immediately struck with such a deadly panic that nothing but confusion and disobedience of orders prevailed among them. The officers in general behaved with incomparable bravery, for which they greatly suffered, there being nearly sixty killed and wounded, a large proportion out of the number we had. Our poor Virginians behaved like men and died like soldiers, for I believe out of three companies that were there that day scarce thirty were left alive. Captain Polson shared almost as hard a fate, for only one of his escaped; in short the dastardly behaviour of the English soldiers exposed all those that were inclined to do their duty to almost certain death, and at length, in despite of every effort, broke and ran like sheep before the hounds, leaving the artillery, ammunition and provisions and every individual thing amongst us as a prey for the enemy; and when we endeavoured to rally them, in hopes of regaining our invaluable loss, it was with as much success as if we had attempted to stop the wild boars on the mountains.

The general was wounded behind the shoulder and in the breast, of which he died the third day after. his two *aids-de-camp* were both wounded, but are in a fair way of recovery. Colonel Burton and Sir John Sinclair were also wounded and I hope will get over it.

Sir Peter Halket, with many other brave officers, was killed on the held. I luckily, escaped without a wound, though I had four bullets through my coat and two horses shot under me.

It is supposed we left 300 or more dead on the field; about that number we brought off wounded, and it is imagined, with great notice too, that two-thirds of both these numbers received their shots from our own cowardly dogs of soldiers who gathered themselves into a body, contrary to orders, ten or twelve deep; would then level and fire and shoot down the men before them.

I tremble at the consequence this defeat may have on the back inhabitants, who I suppose will all leave their habitations unless proper measures are taken for their security. Colonel Dunbar, who commands at present, intends as soon as his men are recruited at this place, to continue his march to Philadelphia into winter quarters, so that there will be none left here unless the poor remains of the Virginia troops who now are and will be too small to guard. our frontier.

As Captain Orme is now writing to your Honour I doubt

not that he will give you a circumstantial account of all things which will make it needless for me to add more than that I am, Honourable Sir,
Your most humble servant,
Geo. Washington.

He then retired to Mt.Vernon, where he arrived on the 26th day of July. Colonel Dunbar returned to England, where in November following he was suspended because of his injudicious retreat, and was sent into honourable retirement as lieutenant governor of Gibraltar. He was never again actively employed, and died in 1777.

By the defeat of Braddock and the withdrawal of the troops the frontiers of Pennsylvania, Maryland and Virginia were left in unutterable gloom. The most westward forts were Fort Cumberland and Fort Ligonier, and behind these the inhabitants shut themselves far east of their western boundaries. This condition of affairs continued until in November, 1758, when Brigadier General John Forbes crossed the mountains at Ligonier and settled forever the dispute for the Ohio Valley.

Some of the Participants

One Samuel Jenkins, who was born a slave and was the property of Captain Broadwater, of Fairfax County, Virginia, drove a provision train over the mountains in the Braddock campaign. He died in Lancaster, Ohio, on the 4th of February, 1849, at the advanced age of 115 years. he doubtless was the last survivor of this ill-fated campaign.

Owen Davis was the owner and driver of a team in this expedition. He settled on Georges Creek, where he built a mill, which he replaced by a far better one in 1795. This mill was erected very near the site of what is recently known as the Ruble mill. Mr. Davis died December 22, 1809, in the 85th year of his age, and was buried on his farm, near the Ruble mill.

Sir John Sinclair was shot through the body and carried to Fort Cumberland. He afterward fully recovered and accompanied General Forbes in his expedition against Fort Duquesne, and the very best eulogy that general could pass upon Sir John was that "his only talent was for throwing everything into contusion." One other accomplishment might have been mentioned, that "he could, on the least provocation, use the vilest and most profane language."

Sir Peter Halket, of Pitcairn, had ominous forebodings as to the result of the coming conflict, and had earnestly pressed upon his general the importance of guarding against an ambuscade. He was captain of the 44th Regiment of Foot and was in command of the First Brigade. In the engagement he was killed from his horse while directing the movements of his men. Two of his sons were fighting under his command, one of which, Lieutenant James Halket, hastened at the moment to his aid, and, bending to raise the prostrate form, he too was pierced by a bullet from the invisible foe and fell dead across the prostrate form of his father.

When Brigadier General John Forbes marched his army out in the fall of 1758 against Fort Duquesne, there accompanied him a son of Sir Peter Halket, who was also Sir Peter Halket, acting at tins time as *aide-de-camp* to General Forbes, a major of the 42nd Regiment. His mission on this occasion to America was principally to ascertain more definitely the fate of his father. In company with other officers of the Highland regiment and a company of Pennsylvania rifles, under Captain West and a few Indians from the neighbourhood who had fought with the French on that fatal day, they proceeded to the scene of the conflict.

One of the Indian guides had seen Sir Peter fall and had also witnessed the sad fate of the son and had no difficulty in identifying the spot. The thick-fallen leaves were removed and the two ghastly skeletons of father and son discovered as they had fallen. Upon examination, young Halket identified the remains of his father by a peculiar artificial tooth and exclaimed "it is my father" and sank into the arms of his scarce less affected companions. The two remains were wrapped in a Highland plaid and interred in a common grave and a volley was fired over their resting places. A stone was placed to mark the sacred spot and the little company marched silently and sadly away. For more than a century that stone remained, to indicate to the visitor of this historic ground the last resting place of one of England's bravest soldiers and Scotland's noblest sons.

Fort Cumberland Continued

After the retirement of the troops under Colonel Dunbar from Fort Cumberland a garrison was still maintained at that post for the protection of the frontier settlers. Colonel James Innes held command there until in May, 1756, when he placed the command with Major James Livingston. Colonel Adam Stephens succeeded Major Livingston in the fall of 1756. About the 1st of February, 1757, Washington, then commander-in-chief of the Virginia forces, established his head-quarters at Fort Cumberland, where he remained until the middle of April, when Captain Dagworthy was placed in command.

Marauding parties of Indians and French continued to harass the frontier, penetrating far eastward of Fort Cumberland, murdering, scalping and plundering even in sight of the walls of the fort. Sieur Langlade, at the head of a detachment of French and Indians, advanced as far as Fort Cumberland in August, 1756, to ascertain the movements of the English, and after reconnoitring the locality retired without doing serious damage. Sieur de Celeron de Blainville, with a scouting party, encountered some English near the fort in August. Three of the English were killed and scalped; de Blainville and three Indians were killed. A detachment under de Celeron penetrated as far as Cresap's Post, some fifteen miles east of Fort Cumberland, and killed eight English.

About the middle of July, 1765, the last British troops were withdrawn from Fort Cumberland, and the frontier settlers were left to their own resources. This state of affairs, happily, was of short duration, as a treaty of peace between the whites and Indians was effected early in 1776.

When what is known as the "Whiskey Insurrection" took place in Western Pennsylvania in 1794, the President ordered out some government troops for its suppression. Some of the troops were quartered for a short time at Fort Cumberland. While here they were inspected by General Washington on the 19th of October, with Generals Lee and Morgan, General Washington appearing in full uniform. This is the last body of troops that ever occupied Fort Cumberland, and is said to be the last time in which Washington appeared in full uniform.

The stone structure, known as the Emmanuel Episcopal church, now occupies a portion of the site of old Fort Cumberland.

General Washington, on his visit to the west in 1784, sought to visit the last resting place of his former commander, through respect for the same, but his search was in vain. He wrote:

> I made diligent search for the grave, but the road had been
> so much turned and the clear land so much extended that
> it could not be found.

Mr. Abraham Stewart, father of the Hon. Andrew Stewart, was road supervisor, and in 1804, while repairing the Braddock road at this place, found human bones a few yards from the road. The military trappings found with them indicated that the remains were those of a British officer of rank and as General Braddock was known to have been buried at this camp the bones doubtless were his. These bones were carefully gathered up and re-interred a short distance eastward from the place they were found, at the foot of an oak tree. Mr. Stewart caused a board to be marked "Braddock's Grave", which was nailed to the tree.

This tree was broken off during a severe storm about 1868. Mr. Josiah King, editor of the *Pittsburgh Gazette*, frequently spent a few weeks' vacation at Chalk Hill, in the vicinity of the grave of General Braddock, and noticing the dilapidated condition of this historic spot, made arrangements to have it enclosed by a neat and substantial fence. In 1872 he procured from Murdock's nursery a willow whose parent stem drooped over the grave of the Emperor Napoleon at St. Helena and planted it over the remains of General Braddock, but unfortunately it soon withered and died. He then planted a number of pine trees within the enclosure, which still remain to indicate to the passer-by the last resting place of Major General Edward Braddock.

The British government has never taken the slightest notice of the spot where sleep the remains of one who gave his service and his life for the English cause. The situation is on the north side and a few yards from the National Road, and a few rods east of where Braddock's run crosses that road, and about nine miles east of Uniontown.

"Far from the land he called his own,
Nor friends nor kindred o'er him weep;
A group of forest trees alone,
Stand sentinels around his keep."

General Braddock's Watch

The gold watch-case of which the above is an illustration was found near the route of Braddock's retreating army in 1880, near a fine spring.

The case is a fine specimen of the engraver's skill and illustrates the legend of "The Judgement of Paris." Paris is represented in a sitting posture; with his right hand he is presenting the golden apple to Venus who stands before him. Beneath his feet are the figures of a dog and a quiver of arrows. Between Paris and Venus is the figure of Cupid. In the rear of Venus are the figures of Hera and Athens, the rivals of Venus. The owl, the helmet, the shield and two peafowls are also represented.

It bears the name of the engraver, George Michael Moser, who excelled in his profession and flourished in the time of Braddock.

The dying general was carried along with the retreating army and doubtless this watch dropped from his pocket and was picked up by one of the frightened soldiers and hidden near a spring expecting some day to recover it, but the opportunity never came.

The works of the watch were corroded away when found and the case is now kept as a relic of that ill-fated expedition.

On July 4th, 1908, a tablet was erected to mark the grave of General Braddock containing the following inscription:

Here lie the mortal remains of
Major General Braddock,

who in command of the Forty-Fourth and Forty-Eighth Regiments of English regulars, was mortally wounded in an engagement with the French and Indians under the command of de Beaujeu at the battle of the Monongahela, within ten miles of Fort Duquesne, July 9, 1755.

He was borne back with the retreating army to the Old Orchard camp, where he died July 13, 1755.

Erected July 4, 1908, under the auspices of the Centennial Celebration committee of 1904.

BRADDOCK'S WATCH

The Site of Braddock's Grave
to be Made a Park

In 1909, a number of spirited citizens of Uniontown, Pa., organized an association to be known as "The General Edward Braddock Memorial Park Association. The officers chosen were Edgar S. Hackney, cashier of the First National Bank, president; James Hadden, secretary and treasurer; and Edgar S. Hackney, James Hadden, W. C. McCormick, Chas. S. Seaton, Isaac W. Semans, E. H. Reppert, J. C. Work, W. A. Stone, and William Hunt, directors.

Twenty-four acres of land, including the grave, have been secured by the association with the purpose of embellishing and preserving this historic spot.

BRADDOCK'S GRAVE

The English Attempt to Drive the French from the Ohio Valley

When France began the erection of a cordon of posts along the Allegheny and Ohio rivers with the purpose of taking possession of the great Mississippi valley, England was aroused to the fact that unless active measures be immediately taken she must forfeit all her claims to this vast and fertile portion of the new world.

English traders had been driven from their trading posts on the Ohio and others had been carried away as prisoners by the French, when Robert Dinwiddie, then governor of the province of Virginia, commissioned George Washington, then just twenty-one years of age, as an envoy to the French posts at the head of the Allegheny River to demand of the commandant of the French forces the purpose of their encroachment upon the territory claimed by the English crown, and to demand his immediate removal.

Being apprised of the intentions of the French, the governor of Virginia immediately dispatched a small force under the command of Captain Trent, Lieutenant Frasher and Ensign Ward, to take possession of the Forks of the Ohio, and to hold the same against the intrusion of the French.

Ward began the construction of a small fort, but before its completion the French dropped down the Allegheny in great numbers and Ward, who was the only officer present at the time, was compelled to surrender without a blow, and retraced his steps to Virginia, and the French began the construction of a fort which they named Fort Duquesne.

At Wills Creek, where the city of Cumberland now stands, Ward was met by Washington, who, in command of a small force, was on his way to the forks with reinforcements.

Washington Fights His First Battle and Defeats the French

On reaching the Great Meadows, fifty-one miles west of Wills Creek, Washington learned that a body of French had been seen not a great distance off, and by the aid of a few friendly Indians under the command of their chief, the Half-King, who were encamped at the Great Rock on the crest of Laurel Hill, he was enabled to surprise them in their secluded encampment. Here an engagement took place at sunrise on the morning of the 28th of May, 1754, in which Jumonville, the commander of the French party, and nine others were killed, one wounded and twenty-one taken prisoners, among whom were M. La Force, M. Drouillion and two cadets; one, a Canadian, escaped.

This was the first battle in which Washington was ever engaged, and was the initial battle of the great French and Indian war.

When the news of the defeat of Jumonville reached Fort Duquesne great activity prevailed and a force was sent against Washington under the command of M. Coulon de Villiers, who was a half-brother to Jumonville. This force came up the Monongahela River in large canoes to the mouth of Redstone Creek, thence passing the place of the engagement: with Jumonville to the Great Meadows, to which place Washington had retreated and erected a small stockade which he named Fort Necessity. Here on the third day of July, 1754, the French forces made an attack, and owing to the distressed condition of his little army,

Washington capitulated; this being the first as well as the last time Washington ever surrendered to a foe.

News of this defeat was soon heralded to England and preparations were immediately made to send two regiments of trained soldiers to recover what the provincial troops had failed to accomplish.

General Braddock Lands
in America

Major General Edward Braddock had entered the British army at the age of fifteen years as a member of the Cold Stream Guards, a very aristocratic division of the army. He was commissioned general-in-chief of His Majesty's forces in North America and arrived at Alexandria in Virginia, February 20, 1755. Two regiments of the royal army, consisting of the Forty-Fourth and Forty-Eighth, to which were added such provincials as might be recruited from Maryland and Virginia were moved against the French at the Forks of the Ohio, where they had erected Fort Duquesne immediately after the surrender of Ward as before mentioned, and thence to Canada.

After a long, tedious and laborious march, consuming more than a month from the time he left Fort Cumberland, General Braddock arrived at the Monongahela River, a short distance below the present town of McKeesport. The army crossed to the left bank of the river; there the manoeuvres of the troops presented the grandest military display Washington claimed it was ever his privilege to behold. The burnished arms of the marching columns flashed in the light of the morning sun as they stepped to the strains of martial music, and the proud British general little thought that within a few short hours these disciplined troops in which he now reposed so much confidence would be fleeing in disorder before a horde of yelling savages.

The army had scarcely recrossed to the right bank of the river, just below the mouth of Turtle Creek, and within ten miles of the fort which they expected to enter in triumph the following day, when a brisk fire was received from an unseen foe. Braddock's troops responded, but to little effect and the engagement which lasted for three hours was most furious.

A Sketch of Thos. Fausett, the Slayer of Major General Edward Braddock, who Became a Resident of Fayette County, Pa.

"Circumstances make strange bedfellows," and it was under peculiar circumstances that the name of Tom Fausett has become inseparably connected with that of the brave officer of the famous Cold Stream Guards, Major General Edward Braddock.

Tom Fausett, the slayer of Braddock, was a large, illiterate, muscular man of great strength, rude habits and strong passions. His brother, Joseph, was doubtless the same, and, as before stated, both were enlisted and served in the same company during the expedition.

When Braddock's retreating army passed over the mountains confusion prevailed and many deserted from the ranks, among whom were Tom and Joe Fausett.

Braddock Meets a Disastrous Defeat

More than half of the army was either killed or wounded, two-thirds of them being shot down by their own men. Braddock had four horses killed under him; at last, while on the fifth, he received a mortal wound which shattered his right arm and penetrated his lungs. He was wrapped in a silken sash taken from about his waist, which English officers were wont to carry, and by his aids, Captain Orme and Captain Stewart of Virginia, assisted by his faithful body servant, Bishop, whom in his dying moments he bequeathed to Washington, he was carried off the field. This silken sash was later presented to General Zachary Taylor and contains woven in its meshes the initials E. B. and is marked with blood stains of that unfortunate general. It was in the possession of Mrs. Bettie Dandridge, the daughter of President Taylor, of Winchester, Va., until her death.

Out of eighty-nine commissioned officers twenty-six were killed and thirty-seven wounded, and of the soldiers four hundred and thirty were killed and about four hundred wounded, the killed being in excess of the wounded. Every field officer and everyone on horseback except Washington, who had two horses killed under him and four bullets through his coat, was either killed or carried off the field wounded. Washington, although enfeebled and emaciated from fever, formed and covered the retreat.

The officers endeavoured in vain to rally the distracted troops, and to intimidate others ran the fugitives through with the sword, and were in turn killed by others. One eye witness declared that the slaughter among the officers was not made by the enemy, but as they had run several fugitives through the body to intimidate the rest, when they were attempting in vain to rally them, some others who expected the same fate fired their pieces with deadly effect.

During the whole of the engagement Braddock raved and swore and cursed his troops as dastards and cowards. The provincials, being acquainted with the Indian mode of warfare, had taken to the trees and were doing good execution, but Braddock ordered them to stand out, as he said, "like English soldiers" and fight in the open. He struck many of them down with his sword, among whom was Joseph Fausett, a brother to the subject of this sketch, and for which act he paid the penalty with his life.

Braddock was described as "desperate in his fortune, brutal in his behaviour and obstinate in his sentiments." His secretary writes of him before the battle

"We have a general most judiciously chosen for being disqualified for the service in which he is employed in almost every respect."

Tom Fausett Fires the Fatal Shot

Thomas Fausett and his brother, Joseph Fausett, were enlisted as privates at six pence a day, at Shippensburg, Pennsylvania, by Captain William Polson, who had served under Washington in the expedition of 1754, into Captain Cholmondeley's company of the 48th Regiment, and marched with the advance of Braddock's army to the fatal field.

During the engagement Tom witnessed the fearful slaughter of the army by the unseen foe, the raving madness of his commander and the striking down of his brother for no other offence than that of fighting in the only successful manner against the Indians. This was too much for a man of his temperament to stand and he determined at once to have revenge and at the same time to put an end to the terrible carnage for which the officers had pleaded in vain. He raised his gun and sent the deadly missile crashing through the right arm and into the lungs of Braddock, who as he fell from his horse expressed the wish that the scene of his defeat might witness his death.

While this rash act of Fausett can never be palliated but deserves hearty condemnation, the affection he had for his brother, the love he bore toward his comrades and countrymen and his admiration for Washington appealed to his untutored mind and brutal instinct more forcibly than his loyalty to his commander.

The wounded commander was borne along with the retreating army until 10 o'clock of the evening of the following day, when they arrived at Gist's plantation, in the exact geographical centre of what is now Fayette county. Here he awaited provisions and hospital stores which he had ordered sent forward from Colonel Dunbar, who was encamped on the summit of Laurel Hill, six miles distant. Braddock still persisted in the exercise of his authority, and on the 11th was removed to Dunbar's camp which he found to be in the utmost confusion. Here he ordered the provisions and ammunition destroyed lest they fall into the hands of the enemy. One hundred and fifty wagons were burned, the powder casks were staved and their contents, to the amount of 50,000 pounds, cast into the stream. Nothing beyond the actual necessities of a flying march was saved, and until recent years this has been a fruitful held for the relic seekers.

General Braddock Dies, and Tom Fausett Locates the Grave Forty-Nine Years Afterward.

On Sunday, the 13th, the army retraced its steps to the Old Orchard Camp where it had halted on its way out. The general softly repeated to himself: "Who would have thought it?" and turning to Orme said, "We shall better know how to deal with them another time." He breathed his last about 8 o'clock on the same night and was wrapped in his cloak as a winding sheet and was buried at daybreak on Monday morning at the camp in the middle of the road that the army in passing over the grave might obliterate every trace of its whereabouts, and thus avoid any desecration of the body by the Indians.

The chaplain having been wounded, Washington read the Episcopal funeral service and the dead general was buried in the honours of war. Abraham Stewart, father of the late Honourable Andrew Stewart, was road supervisor in Wharton township in 1804, and while repairing the old road at this place Tom Fausett, who had settled in this neighbourhood after the retreat of the army, as will be related hereafter, came along where the men were at work and remarked, "If you will dig right there," indicating, "you will find the bones of General Braddock," and sure enough, Mr. Stewart dug as directed and exhumed the bones of the unfortunate general and his military trappings.

A merchant happened to witness the discovery and carried

off one of the largest bones which he placed in Peale's museum in Philadelphia where it was destroyed by fire. Mr. Stewart carefully re-interred the remainder of the bones at a short distance east of the place where they were found, at the foot of an oak tree and caused a board to be marked "Braddock's Grave", which was nailed to the tree. This tree was broken off in a severe storm about 1868. Mr. James Mitchell, a blacksmith, who lived at Mt. Washington, and Mr. Peter Hager, who was raised in the family of Mr. Stewart, with others witnessed the re-interment of Braddock's remains and often related the circumstances to others.

Mr. Josiah King, editor of the *Pittsburgh Gazette*, frequently spent a few weeks' vacation at Chalk Hill in the vicinity of the grave of General Braddock, and noticing the dilapidated condition of this historic spot, made arrangements with Mr. Dixon, the proprietor of the land, to have it enclosed with a neat and substantial fence. In 1872, he procured from Murdock's nursery a willow whose parent stem drooped over the grave of the Emperor Napoleon at St. Helena and planted it over the remains of General Braddock, but, unfortunately it soon withered and died. He then planted a number of pine trees within the enclosure which still remain to indicate to passers-by the last resting place of the unfortunate general.

The British government has never taken the slightest notice of the spot where sleep the remains of one who gave his service and his life for the English cause.

> "Far from the land he called his own,
> Nor friends nor kindred o'er him weep;
> A group of forest trees alone
> Stand sentinels around his keep."

The situation is on the north side and a few yards from the National Road and a few rods east of where Braddock's Run crosses that road, about nine miles east of Uniontown.

Washington's Springs, on the Crest of Laurel Hill Once Owned by Tom Fausett.

The next we learn of Tom Fausett we find him located on the summit of Laurel Hill at the junction of Dunlap's Road, which led to the Monongahela River at the mouth of Dunlap's Creek, with the Braddock Road, which here turned abruptly to the north and on to Gist's and to Stewart's Crossing of the Youghiogheny River a short distance below the present town of Connellsville.

This location has always been known as Washington's Springs and was on a tract of 102¾ acres of land which was warranted the 17th of September, 1772, to Henry Hunt. Here Fausett conducted a tavern for some years, besides spending much of his time in hunting the wild game so abundant in those days. A writer in the National Intelligencer, supposed to have been the late William Darby, Esq., said: When my father was removing with his family to the west one of the Fausetts kept a public house eastward from Uniontown, with whom we lodged about the 10th of October, 1781, and there it was made anything but a secret that he dealt the death blow to the British General.

Thirteen years afterwards, 1794, I again met Tom Fausett and put to him the plain question, "Did you shoot General Braddock?" and his reply was prompt and explicit.

"I did shoot him," and then went on to explain that by so

doing he had contributed to save what was left of the army. The property rolls of Wharton township give Tom Fausett as located here and having in his possession horses and cows as taxables. How Fausett acquired the right to this tract is not apparent, but on April 29th, 1788, he disposed of it as the following abstract from the public records will show:

"Know all men by these presents, that I, Thomas Fausett, of the county of Phayette and state of Pennsylvania for and in consideration of the sum of fifty pounds to me in hand paid by Isaac Philips of the same place the receipt whereof I do acknowledge have granted, bargained, sold, released, confirmed and made over all my rite tract of land and parcel of land I now live upon at the forks of the road on the top of Laurel Hill known by the name of Washington's Spring adjoining the lands of Jonathan Hill Els whereby vacant land containing one hundred acres more or less to have and to hold the said tract of land and premises and appurtenances thereunto belonging unto the said Isaac Phillips his heirs and assigns warranting and defending it all. Every of myself my heirs or any claim or claiming by virtue of my rite and title to said land only nevertheless under and subject to the states and it all other dues and demands unto which the same are liable.

"In witness whereof I have set my hand and seal hereunto. Dated the 29th day of April in the year of our Lord one thousand seven hundred eighty eight.

"his Thomas X Fosset, seal mark."

A few years after Fausett had disposed of his claim to the Washington's Springs tract it came into the possession of John Slack who had previously kept a tavern in Uniontown. Slack's tavern stood some little distance south of the Washington's Springs and here he conducted his business for many years. This was a favourite stopping place and was extensively known and patronized by the wagoners on the old road. His daughter, Tamzon, married Ephraim McClean who kept a public house on the summit of Laurel Hill in the palmy days of the old National Road. Slack's place was considered a good stand for the entertainment of the travelling public until the completion of the National Road, at which time the old Braddock Road was abandoned and quiet once more settled over the old Nemacolin Trail.

Tom Fausett was said to have been married three times and that two of his wives were killed by the Indians, and that his favourite, as he termed her his "little Dutch wife," was tomahawked before his eyes. There is no tradition in this section of the country that he had a wife after settling here, but after retiring from the tavern business and disposing of his tract of land he remained a citizen of Wharton township, and for some time occupied a cabin on the old Braddock road back of Chalk Hill. This old cabin was west of what was long known as the Cushman House, the location of which is still visible, and still west of his old cabin is a group of immense rocks known as the "Peddler's Rocks."

With this picturesque group of rocks is connected the legend that at one time a peddler was murdered here for his money and pack of jewellery and other valuables which he carried. His pack and other articles were found secreted among these rocks, but what became of the peddler was never certainly known, but suspicion rested upon more than one of the several persons living in the neighbourhood of the rocks.

While Tom Fausett occupied this old cabin, making a precarious living with his gun, he had as his housekeeper an old coloured woman who had been a slave. One morning upon calling his house-keeper and receiving no response he went to her couch and found her cold in death. She was buried in a field some distance away between two apple trees, as markers, and as there was no minister present to conduct the funeral service one of the neighbours deeming it appropriate that some remarks should be made at the grave, ventured the following:

"Earth to earth and dust to dust,
If the Lord won't take her the devil must."

WASHINGTON'S SPRINGS

PEDDLER'S ROCKS

Joseph Fausett, although struck down with the sword of the enraged Braddock, survived, and also became a resident of Wharton township, and left descendants. One of his sons, Joseph Fausett, Jr., married Amelia Lynch, daughter of Cornelius Lynch of Uniontown, who at one time owned and occupied the ground now covered by the Thompson-Ruby building, corner Main and Morgantown streets. This son, Joseph, owned a farm north of Chalk Hill and died young, leaving a wife and two small children, Joseph and Elizabeth, the latter of whom is well remembered by the older citizens of Uniontown. The widow, as administratrix, sold the farm, September 28th, 1800, to John Chaplin who in turn conveyed the same to Jonathan Downer. Another son of the original Joseph Fausett was Uriah who left quite a family of which one daughter, Rebecca, made her home in Wharton township until old age overtook her when she was sent to the county home, to which institution she was admitted May 17, 1906, and where she died Jan. 9, 1910, aged 84 years, having made her home for more than forty years with William Smith and was later the housekeeper of Isaac Spiker a short distance east of Farmington.

Tom Fausett Confesses that He Fired the Fatal Shot that Killed Braddock

Tom Fausett never denied that he fired the shot that killed Braddock, but upon repeated occasions, especially when in his cups, did he relate the circumstances which prompted him to commit the deed. besides the confessions already recited, Mr. Freeman Lewis, who assisted Judge Veech in collecting data in compiling his *Monongahela of Old*, recites that he at one time taught a country school and one day when the children were at play he heard the cry of "There's old Tom Fausett, the man who killed Braddock." The children feared him, his appearance and noisiness, especially when intoxicated, being rather terrifying. I knew him and got him to sit down by a tree. He at once began fluttering his fingers over his mouth to imitate the roll of a drum, he soon got at his old rigmarole, which ran about thus:

> Poor fellows—poor fellows they are all gone—murdered by a madman—Braddock was a madman—he would not let us tree, but made us stand out and be shot down when we could see no Indians;—Yes, Braddock was a madman. He said, 'No skulking, no treeing, but stand out and give them fair English play.' If he had been shot when the battle began and Washington had taken command we would have licked them,—yes, we'd a licked them.

"How could you have done that?" I asked.

"Why, we'd 'ave charged on them, and driven them out of

the brush and pea-vines,—then we would have seen their red skins and could have peppered them—yes, we'd have peppered their red skins."

He would then repeat his "boo-oo-oo my old Virginia Blues—poor fellows—all gone," &c, &c., and tears would roll over his rough cheeks.

Fausett often related the circumstances of the killing of Braddock to the late Honourable Andrew Stewart, who served eighteen years in congress, who when a young man and a resident of Wharton township was intimately acquainted with Fausett, then in his old age. Peter Hager, who was raised as a member of the family of Abraham Stewart, and who assisted in removing the bones of General Braddock, repeatedly heard Fausett relate the circumstances of the killing of what he termed the madman.

The late Basil Brownfield of South Union township, who was born near the present site of Smithfield, related that Tom Fausett frequently visited that locality on hunting expeditions, and that by frequent interviews with him he learned that the Fausetts were at one time residents of the South Branch valley, in the present state of West Virginia, from the neighbourhood of the site of Moorefield, and that Tom's principal occupation was that of a hunter.

One time on returning from a hunting expedition he was horrified at finding his cabin in ashes and the dead and scalped bodies of his wife and children a short distance off where they had been overtaken and slaughtered by the Indians. He could never refer to this incident without manifesting great emotion and tears would roll down his rugged cheeks. He said he could not remain in the vicinity where his family had been killed, and removed to Pennsylvania where he and his brother enlisted in Braddock's campaign.

Mr. Brownfield further related that Fausett was a man of rugged frame, of uninviting features, distant in his manners, rarely associating with others, was not communicative when sober but inclined to be boisterous and boastful when intoxicated. He frequently related to Mr. Brownfield that he fired the fatal shot at

Braddock in revenge for striking his brother and for other offences.

It is related that an Indian trader by the name of McCullough used to travel an Indian trail leading from Winchester to the west and the trail became known as McCullough's path. This McCullough was in the habit of supplying the Indians, even in times of war, with knives, hatchets, powder and balls. The settlers threatened him for this but he would not desist. Learning when he was to pass that way a number of settlers disguised themselves and went in pursuit. They caught and threatened him with dire punishment unless he gave up his nefarious traffic. He at first refused to comply with their wishes, but Tom Fausett, being one of the party, caught McCullough in his giant grasp and held him until his tormentors made him promise never more to transgress, and after despoiling him of his peltry, they let him go, and he never was seen again in that region of country.

Writers upon this unfortunate expedition are wont to cast a doubt as to the manner in which Braddock received his death wound, and produce conflicting rumours to dispute the statements made by Fausett. No one who was acquainted with Fausett, knew his disposition and habits, doubted his statement as to the death of the British general. Freeman Lewis, previously referred to, stated that his last interview with Fausett was in the month of October, 1816,. and that Fausett then claimed to be one hundred and four years of age, and that his appearance bore him out, and that some of Fausett's statements were "wholly irreconcilable with well ascertained facts." Who would expect an illiterate man at that extreme age to relate circumstances in detail with perfect accuracy that had transpired a half century before?

Winthrop Sargent in his *Braddock's Expedition* goes some length to disprove the statements made by Fausett, while at the same time he adduces the evidence of William Butler who had served as a private in the Pennsylvania Greens at the defeat of Braddock, and under Forbes in 1758, and under Wolf in 1759, at the Plains of Abraham, who when interrogated as to the killing of Braddock unhesitatingly declared that he was shot by Fausett for striking down his brother. The *Millerstown* (Perry county, Pa.) *Gazette* of 1830, mentions the fact that Butler was in that town in company with another who had served under Braddock and that both concurred in saying that Braddock had been killed by Fausett.

The *Colonization Herald* (Philadelphia) of June 20. 1838, contained the notice of the death of William Butler at the age of one hundred and eight years, and further states that he had lived at the corner of Sixth and Chestnut streets, which was then in woods and leaning on his crutch, often entertained visitors by a recital of the unfortunate expedition and the circumstances of the death of Braddock.

The evidence of Billy Brown, a negro living at Frankfort, Pennsylvania, taken in 1826, when he was ninety-three years of age is also adduced to confirm Fausett's story. He was born in Africa and brought as a slave to this country at an early age. He was present at Braddock's defeat as a servant to a colonel in the Irish regiment. He relates that Braddock's character was obstinate and profane and he also confirms the report that Braddock was shot by an American because he had killed, or was supposed to have killed, his brother, and that none seemed to care for it.

Daniel Adams of Newberryport, Massachusetts, states that in 1842, it had been told him by one who had it from another who was present at the occurrence that the principal officers had desired a retreat which the general pertinaciously refused and upon seeing the rashness of the commander a brother of one who had been stricken down fired the fatal shot, which several of the soldiers witnessed but said nothing.

Historian Sargent in his effort to disprove that Braddock met his death at the hands of Fausett not only admits but certainly establishes the fact that such was the current belief at the time among those in position to know.

A still further witness who heretofore has entirely escaped the notice of the historian is James Edwards, who was a captain in one of the Associated Companies of Kent County, now Dela-

Rebecca Fausett, Grand-daughter of Joseph Fausett

ware, in August, 1748, in the service of the Province of Pennsylvania. He enlisted in Braddock's campaign, and in the defeat was wounded in the leg by a musket ball, which he carried to his grave. He subsequently served in the Revolutionary war in Colonel Thomas Proctor's celebrated artillery in preference to infantry on account of his wounded leg, and served at Brandywine, Chadd's Ford, Newtown, Germantown, Bergen Neck and Trenton. Mr. Edwards finally settled at Barnegat, New Jersey, where he was a prominent member of the Methodist Episcopal Church.

He too lived to an advanced age and frequently related the scenes of Braddock's defeat and always positively asserted that the unfortunate general was killed by one of his own men by the name of Fausett for striking down his brother and, as he thought, uselessly sacrificing the lives of his soldiers. Mr. Edwards was an ardent admirer of Washington and in his old age expressed his willingness to depart and join his "dear old General, Washington," whom he believed to be one of the brightest stars in the region of glory. Mr. Edwards is buried in the Methodist Church yard at Tuckerton, New Jersey.

It will be remembered that Braddock's army precipitately fled from the fatal field and scattered like leaves before the hurricane, but Sargent does not account for the fact that William Butler, of Philadelphia, and Billy Brown of Frankfort, Pennsylvania and Daniel Adams of Newberryport, Massachusetts, and James Edwards of New Jersey, and many others, having no communication whatever with each other all concurred in relating substantially the same story as Fausett unless they had gotten these facts before the army was disbanded at Fort Cumberland on the retreat.

The evidence here adduced is certainly all that would be necessary to warrant conviction in a court of justice were Fausett on trial for having fired the fatal shot at the British general.

Tom Fausett Becomes a Charge Upon the Township of Wharton

For some years before his death Tom Fausett became a charge upon the township of Wharton, and it was the custom to sell out paupers to the lowest bidder. In an old book still extant, kept by the overseers of the poor for that township, are the following entries:

March 20, 1812, Be it remembered that James Wear has undertaken to keep Thomas Fausett for the space of one year for the sum of thirty-seven dollars and seventy-five cents exclusive of finding him any clothing.

March 19, 1813, Samuel Spaugh undertakes to keep Thomas Fausett one year for the sum of thirty-seven dollars and seventy-five cents, exclusive of finding him any clothing.

April 4, 1814, For the keeping of Fausett for one year, fifty-seven dollars. For selling Fausett in 1814, $1.00.

For the keeping of Fausett for the year

March 15, 1816, Be it remembered that Thomas Mitchell undertakes to keep Thomas Fausett, one of the poor of Wharton township, for one year for forty-eight dollars exclusive of finding him clothing.

March 21, 1817, Be it remembered that Edward Tissue undertakes to keep Thomas Fausett, one of the poor of Wharton township, exclusive of finding him clothing, for one year for $37.50.

March 20, 1818, Be it remembered that Thomas Mitchell undertakes to keep Thomas Fausett, one of the poor of Wharton township, exclusive of finding him clothing for twenty-eight dollars and fifty cents, the time not to commence until the 24th of April.

April 24, 1819, Be it remembered that Thomas Mitchell undertakes to board, lodge and wash and mend and find tobacco for Thomas Fausett for one year from this date for the sum of fifty dollars.

Auditors report for 1819. By noticing the sale of Fausett for the present year, fifty cents, tobacco for Fausett, twenty-five cents, paid for keeping Fausett twenty-eight dollars and fifty cents.

April 24, 1819. By one day selling Fausett and settling with auditors, $1.00.

1820, Contra. Moses Mercer and John Bolin, overseers of the poor, Cr. by keeping Thomas Fausett, fifty dollars.

By Fausett clothing and Mercer, his attendance, sixty-two dollars and seventy-five cents.

From this last entry it would appear that poor old Tom had been deprived of clothing until he had no further use of the same. Then the township furnished a suit in order that he might appear the more respectable in the happy hunting grounds.

This last entry in this old township book would indicate that Tom Fausett died in 1820, and that Moses Mercer was in attendance at his death and burial, and that the overseers of the poor settled the bill of expenses. From the fact that Fausett's name does not again appear on the book the inference would be reasonable that he died during the year 1820.

For some years before his death Fausett made his home in a little log cabin which stood on what was subsequently the Frederick Nicolay farm about one mile and a hail west of Ohiopyle Falls. Here he cultivated among other things a little patch of tobacco for his own use which he husbanded with the greatest care. This old cabin, like its tenant, has long since passed away,

GRAVE OF THOMAS FAUSETT

but after nearly a half century had rolled away since the death of its distinguished occupant, Mr. Nicolay was plowing near the site of the old cabin, a few stones of the old chimney only remaining, near which his plow turned up a small box containing a quantity of silver coins and jewellery. He took his find to Pittsburgh for the purpose of ascertaining its value, the coins being in different denominations of foreign money such as was current in those early days, and placed it in charge of an old acquaintance and well known banker of that city, but notwithstanding his frequent inquiries he died before he ascertained the value or recovered his valuable discovery.

The finding of this box of jewellery and coin revived the story that was current in the mountain region of Wharton township many years before, as previously related, that a peddler had been murdered at the Peddler's Rocks near the cabin of Fausett, and the discovery of this box with its peculiar contents would indicate that Fausett might have known somewhat of the missing peddler.

Fausett's last home was in the family of Thomas Mitchell, about two miles west of Ohiopyle Falls. He was buried in a small burying ground on what was known as the Jacob H. Rush farm, since occupied by the late Patton Rush, where also rest the remains of many of the old residents of that neighbourhood. Some years after his death a rude headstone was erected to his memory on which is inscribed the following:

Tho. Faucet
died March 23
1822
Aged 109
9 mos

Thus is marked the last resting place of the slayer of Major General Edward Braddock, and on each recurring memorial day a flag and a few flowers are placed on the little mound of earth to keep his memory green.

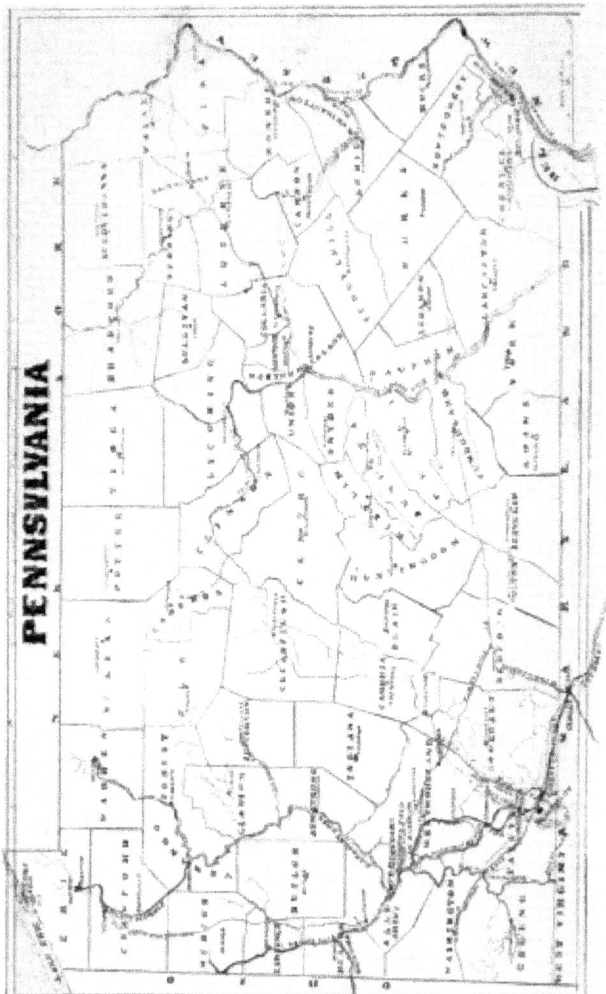
PENNSYLVANIA

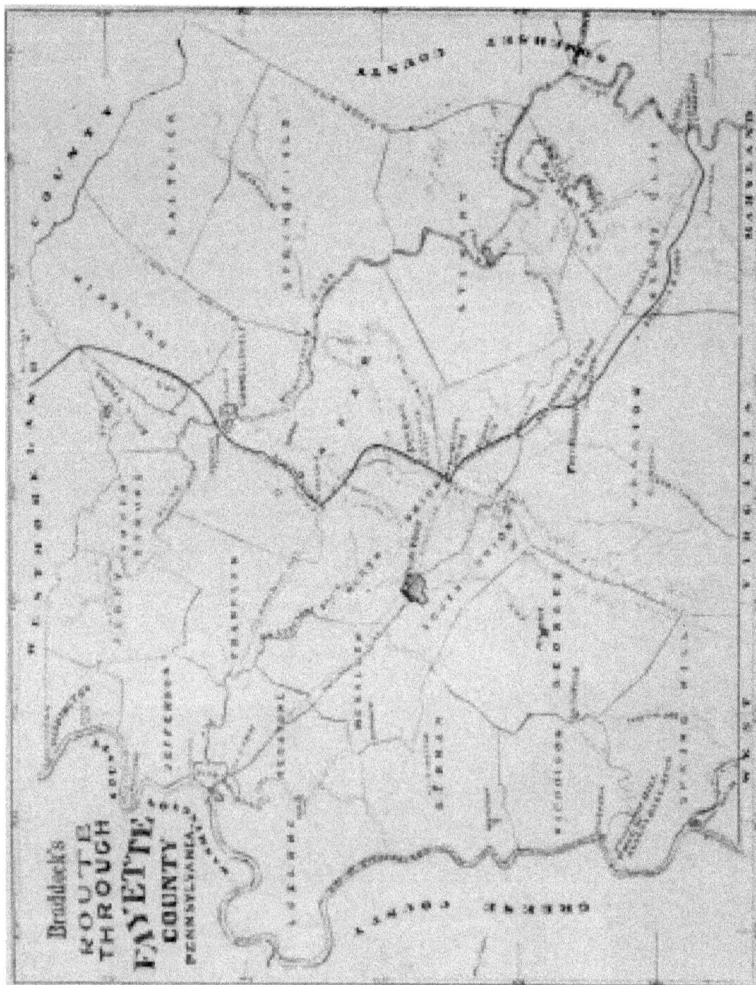

Braddock's
ROUTE
THROUGH
FAYETTE
COUNTY
PENNSYLVANIA

Braddock's Orderly Book

Contents

Major General Edward Braddock's Orderly Book From February 26 To June 17, 1755

What immediately follows, is the orders of his Excellency General Braddock from his arrival in Virginia until the 17th of June following, when indisposition obliged the writer, or copier, thereof to seperate from him and remain (until he was in a condition to move forward again) with the rear division of the army. Rejoining in a low and enfeebled state, only the day before the Action of Monnongalia (which happened on the 9th of July) there was not time even if he had been able to enter the orders that had issued during his seperation; which is more to be regretted as it is probable the order of battle, and many other important orders were among them.

He did, however, as may be seen by a letter to Captain Orme, dated the 28th day of July—Request a copy of these orders, but as they never were sent, they cannot be inserted.

(General Braddock's orderly books are two in number, the first embracing the orders issued from the 26th, of February to the 11th of June, 1755; and the second from the 12th to the 17th of June, 1755. On a page preceding the orders appears the above extract, in Washington's own handwriting, and it is presumed that the books were kept under his direction. These books were transferred to the Congressional Library from the library of the late Peter Force, after the death of that eminent man, whose collection of manuscripts concerning American history was un-doubtedly the most complete in existence.)

General Braddock's Orderly Book, No. 1.

His Excellency General Braddock orders that the commanding officer of each ship upon their arrival in Hamptom Road shall immediately send a return inclosed to Mr. Hunter at Hampton, specifying the number of their sick, the time of their illness, and the nature of them. And that every commanding officer shall with the utmost dispatch apply to Mr. Hunter for boats to carry the sick on shore which shall be executed with all imaginable care and expedition, and that a subaltern officer of each ship shall see their men safely conveyed to the place appointed at Hampton for their reception, which Mr. Hunter will shew them; and that the surgeons or mates of the two regiments and train shall attend the sick of their own corps. Every commanding officer is to take particular care that as soon as their sick are sent a shore all the hatchways be uncovered, scuttles opened and the platform thoroughly washed and cleaned, no officer or soldier, except the sick, to lie on shore upon any acct. The hospital to continue on board till the general s further orders.

Williamsburg, February 26th, 1755.

To the companies of Rangers and carpenters:

His Excellency General Braddock orders the commanding officer of each company or troop to send a weekly return to the headquarter s agreeable to the form annexed; and duplicates of the returns are to be remitted weekly to His Excellency, Governor Dinwiddie. The return for General Braddock to be directed to me at the headquarters.

Williamsburg February 26th, 1755.

By His Excellency Edward Braddock, Esq.:

Whereas, an act of Parliament was passed in England, the last session, to subject all troops raised in the colonies to the regulations and orders of the articles of war, I therefore think it expedient and order that upon forming the four companies of rangers, the company of carpenters and the troops of light horse and whatever troops are or shall be raised for the service of the present expedition. That the articles of war be publickly read to the officers and men, and that every man severaly shall take the Oath of Allegiance and supremacy; and in consequence of these articles they are to obey from time to time any orders they shall receive from me or any of their superior officers.

E. Braddock,

by His Excellencys Commanded.

February. 26th, 1755.   William Shirley, Secretary.

By His Excellency Edward Braddock, Esq., General Commander in Chief of His Majesty's Forces in North America, quarters of Sir Peter Halket's Regiment:

Ordered, that it proceed to Alexandria in the transports; five companies to remain in the town with the company of artillery and stores of all kinds.

One company at Dumfries, two days march from Alexandria, thirty miles to halt the first night after they cross the ferry of Occoquan; One company at Bladensburg, one days march, they cross the Potomack at Alexandria; One company at upper Marlborrough two days march first night at Bladensburg; Two companys at Frederick; These three last cantonments in Maryland; upon application to Major Carlyl magistrate of Alexandria, the whole will be furnished with guides quarters of one regiment. The transports which have them on board to stop in the River Potomack as near Fredericksburg as they can; These and an halt company at Winchester, six days march from Fredericksburg, halt a company at Conogogee eight days from Winchester; six companys at Fredericksburg and Falmouthon the other side the River of Rappahaunock.

The five companys of the regiment that disembark at Alexandria which are to be canton d to be landed first and to begin their march before the other five debark.

The engineers and other officers, not immediately wanted to be at hand, may be conveniently lodged on the Maryland side of the Potomack leaving a direction where they lodge.

Application is to be made to the several magistrates tor carriages to convey the stores, baggage and tents of the cantoned companys to be given by the commanding officers for the numbers employed.

The regiment whose headquarters are at Fredericksburg, will halt about fifteen miles from place of disembarking. Waggons will be ordered to attend them. Three companys which are to march to Winchester and Conogogee are to march first to Fredericksburg. The company quartered at Falmouth need not cross the Rappa. Waggons to each company to be assertained, a field officer to go with each of the five companys and every officer to go with his company.

Given under my hand at Williamsborg, this 28th February, 1755.

E. Braddock.

Camp at Alexandria,
Thursday 27th March, 1755.
Parole Williamsburg.

Captain Robert Orme of the Coldstream Regiment of Guards, and Captain Roger Morris of Colonel Dunbar's regiment of foot, are appointed *aids de camp* to His Excellency General Braddock.

His Majesty has been pleased to appoint Captain Halket, of Sir Peter Halket's regiment; brigade major.

As the troops have taken the field His Excellency General Braddock is desirous the officers and men should be informed of the duties he requires of them, and of some regulations he thinks beneficial to the service: and as the two regiments now employed have served under the command of His Royal Highness and are well acquainted with military discipline, His Excellency expects their conduct will be so conformable to order as to set the most soldier like example to the new service of this country; and the general orders that the articles of war be immediately and frequently read, and that everybody may be informed all neglects or disobedience of them or any orders will not be forgiven.

Any soldier who shall desert though he return again will be hanged without mercy.

As an incouragement to the men, and to promote their diligence and activity, every man will be allowed daily as much of fresh or salt provision, and of bread or flower without any stoppages for the same as long and in as great proportions as it will be possible to provide them unless any man shall be found drunk, negligent, or disobedient, in such case his gratuity shall be stopped.

All orders relating to the men are constantly to be read to them by an officer of the company.

The eldest captain's company of each regiment is to act as a second grenadier's company and to be posted upon the left of the battalion, leaving the same interval as the grenadiers upon the right; This company is to be kept compleat of officers and two of them as well as of the other grenadier company are to be posted in the front and the other in the rear.

The eight battallian companies are to form so many firings and to be commanded by their respective officers. The commanding officer of each company is to give the word, the second is to be posted in the center of the front rank and the remaining subaltern officers of the regiment after this disposition are to divide the ground equally: These firings are to begin by the colonel's company, second by the lieutenant colonels and continued from right to left as fast as possibly, but the two captains of grenadiers are to take particular care never to give their fire till the companys upon the right and left are loaded .

To avoid confusion if the regiment should be ordered to wheel or fire by platoons, every officer commanding a company is to tell it off in two divisions and to post the second commissioned officer and non commissioned officers, and when the regiment decamps or are to form, the commanding officer of the company is to instruct his men's arms, compleat the files, post the officers and see his men loaded that they may wheel up and ye battalion be instantly formed.

The officers upon a march are to remain in the same order with their companies, and those officers who were placed in the rear are to march as posted which will consequently be upon the flank as the regiment moves by files they are therefore required to keep the soldiers in their files, and if any lag behind one or more of these officers is to bring them up.

Every officer leaving his company upon a march will be cashiered, and every commanding officer will be answerable for the men of his company left behind; and the commanding officer of the regiments are ordered to punish with the utmost severity any soldier who leaves his file but in cases of sickness.

Commanding officers of companies are to have their arms in constant good order, and every man to be provided with a brush, picker, two good spare flints and twenty-four cartridges.

The roll of each company to be called by a commissioned officer, morning, noon and night, and a return of the absent or disorderly men to be given to the commanding officer of the regiment who is to order proper punishment.

The women of each regiment are to march with the provost and none upon any account are to appear with the men when under arms.

Each regiment is to mount a piquet guard consisting of one captain and three subalterns and 100 men to be paraded at the retreat they are to report to the field officer of the day.

The two regiments are to find the general's guard alternately consisting of one lieutenant, and thirty private and report to an *aid de camp*. The regiment which finds the guard finds also the adjutant of the day.

All guards are to be retired at 8 o'clock; all guards to be told of in two divisions though ever so small.

Guards ordered at orderly time are to remain for that duty and a new detachment is to be made for any ordered afterwards.

All returns are to be signed by the commanding officer of regiments. Reports of all guards except the general's are to be made to the field officer of the day who is to visit them once at least and to go the piquet rounds.

All remarkable occurrances in camp to be reported to an *aid de camp*.

Returns of all commands to be made to the brigade major, and every regiment, company, troop, &c., are to make a daily return to him specifying the numbers wanting to compleat, who is to make one general return to his Excellency.

A daily return of the sick is to be made to the general through an *aid de camp*.

As the nature of the country make it impossible to provide magazines of forage, and as it is apprehended the quantity will be very small, uncertain, and difficult to be procured His Excellency recommends it to all the officers to take no more baggage than they find absolute occasion for.

Commanding officers of regiments are directed by His Excellency to inform their men not to suffer themselves to be alarmed upon a march by any stragling fires from the Indians in the woods, they being of no consequence nor liable to any inconveniences but what arise from their misbehaviour.

Any soldier by leaving his company, or by words or gestures expressing fear shall suffer death and the general will greatly approve and properly reward those men who by their coolness and good discipline treat the attempt of these fellows with the contempt they deserve.

The sergents of the two regiments are to be provided with firelocks and bayonets, but to wear their swords They are to leave at Winchester under the care of the train their halters and all the private men their swords. His Excellency likewise recommends it to all the officers to provide themselves if possible with fuzeis, as espontoons will be extreamely inconvenient and useless in the woods.

As the good of the service renders the presence of all the officers absolutely necessary His Excellency cannot suffer any commissioned officer to act as pay master, the general therefore desires the colonels and captains will agree as soon as possible for a proper person for that purpose.

The line is to find one field officer daily to be relieved at 10 o'clock, this duty to be done by the two lieutenant colonels and two majors, the field officer, is to visit all the guards except the general's and to go the rounds of the picquet which as well as other guards and posts are to report to the field officer and he is to make his report of ye whole at nine o'clock every morning to the general and in case of any alarm the field officer is to repair to the place of alarm with all expedition and to send for all necessary assistance to the two regiments who are immediately to comply with his orders.

All reports and returns to be made before nine o clock, all out posts are to receive the general with shouldered arms and without beat of drum or salute.

Upon any application from Sir John St Clair quartermaster general for men the regiments are immediately to furnish them.

Sir Peter Halket is to be applied to for all regulations of provisions and his orders are to be strictly complied with.

All guards are to rest and beat two ruffles to his Honour Governor Dinwiddie.

The regiments are to hold themselves in readiness for a muster, each company is to provide their rolls one of parchment, and those officers with new commissions are to have them in their pockets, after the muster the general will receive the two regiments by companys the officers to be in boots and the men in brown gaters.

The adjutants of the two regiments and artillery, and also the adjutant of the Rangers to be at the major of brigade's tent, every day at eleven o'clock to receive orders.

A sergeant from the two regiments artillery and rangers to attend the major of brigade as orderly, and to be relieved every day at guard mounting.

The gentlemen of the hospital and their servants are to receive tomorrow three days' provisions. field officers for the day Lieutenant Colonel Gage.

Alexandria, March 28th, 1755.

Parole Albemarle.

The general's guard to be mounted in brown gaters, and the officers in boots.

Sir Peter Halket's Colonel Dunbar's and the Royal Regiment of Artillery are to be mustered, on Monday morning at seven o clock, and afterwards they will be received by General Braddock.

Robert Webster of Sir Peter Halket's regiment is appointed provost marshal and he is to be obeyed accordingly.

One sergeant; one corporal and twelve men to mount as a guard for the provost marshal and be relieved every forty-eight hours.

The adjutant who does not send in his return to the major of brigade, by seven o'clock in the morning will be ordered under an arrest.

The quartermaster of the corps which is to receive provisions is to give to the commissary a signed return of the number he is to draw provisions for every Saturday at six in the afternoon: The quarter masters of the different corps are to give into Sir Peter Halket's a return of the provisions they delivered out that week, distinguishing the quantitys delivered each corps; in this return he is to have columns for the quantitys of each species of provisions he has received that week and a column for the quantitys remaining in store.

Tomorrow at orderly time the adjutants are to deliver in a return of the number of served who are not soldiers and for whom provisions are to be drawn for; The commissary are to make two copys of this return, one for General Braddock, the other for Sir Peter Halket.

Field officer tomorrow Lieutenant Colonel Burton. For the generals guard 48th Regiment.

One of the orderly sergeants or the major of brigade is to carry the orders to Sir John St. Glair.

A general court martial consisting of one field officer, six captains and six subalterns, to sit tomorrow morning at 8 o'clock.

Lieutenant Colonel Gage, President. Sir Peter Halkett gives three captains and three subalterns; Colonel Dimbar gives three captains and three subalterns. Mr. Shirley Judge Advocate; The picquet to consist of one captain, two subalterns and fifty men till further orders. No officer, soldier or any other person to fire a gun within a mile round the camp.

Camp at Alexandria, March 29th, 1755.

Parole—Boston.

For the General Guard 44th Regiment.

The alarm post for all the Virginian troops quartered in the town of Alexandria to be before the march.

When any man is sent to the general hospital he is to bring a certificate signed by an officer, of his name. Regiment and company, to what day he is subsisted, and what arms and acoutrements he brings with him. The arms and accoutrements to be bundled up, and marked, with the man's name and company

Colonel Dunbar's regiment tomorrow to receive three days provisions.

On Sunday every regiment in camp, is to have divine service at the head of their colours.

AFTER ORDERS.

Each regiment to send to the train for twenty thousand flints out of which number, they are to pick five thousand, and to send the remainder back again; the commanding officers giving their receipts for what number s they receive.

All the Virginia troops that are quartered in Alexandria to be under arms, tomorrow morning at half an hour after seven o clock.

The officers that were formerly appointed pay masters, to continue so till further orders and are to issue out in payment to the troops, each a dollar at 4 c |9 shilling.

When either regiment have occasion for ammunition, or any military stores the commanding officers are to send to the artillery when they will be supplied giving their receipts accordingly.

The general court martial where of Lieutenant Colonel Gage was President is dissolved, and James Anderson of Colonel Dunbar's regiment who was tryed by ye general court martial is ordered 1,000 lashes with a cat and nine tails which he is to receive in such manner as the commanding officer shall think proper.

Field officer for tomorrow, Lieutenant Colonel Gage.

Camp at Alexandria, 30th March, 1755.
Parole—"Chichester."

The two regiments are to be mustered tomorrow morning at seven o'clock but the general will not receive the troops till further orders.

The two regiments from Ireland are to act for their men for their sea pay giving them credit for their subsistence to the first of March and for their arms to the 24th of February; The captains are to take credit for their watch coats, blankets and flannell waistcoats brought from Great Britain for their companys.

The men listed or incorporated into Sir Peter Halket's, and Colonel Dunbar's regiment are to have credit for twenty shillings and to be charged with the above mentioned necessarys His Excellency orders this to be taken from the recruiting fund, and gives it to those men for their incouragement that they may do their duty like good soldiers.

The first company of carpenters are to march tomorrow morning to Sir John St Clair for further orders.

A return to be sent tomorrow morning to Sir John St Clair from Sir Peter Halket's and Colonel Dunbar's regiments of the number of draughts they have received by whom they were enlisted and from what company's draughted.

Camp at Alexandria, 31st of March, 1755.
Parole—Darlington.
Field officer for tomorrow. Lieutenant Colonel Burton. For the General's Guard 44th Regiment.

All casualties or occurrances that happen in camp to be reported immediately to the general through an *aid de camp*.

Whenever Sir John St Clair has occasion for artificers tools, or implements he is to apply to the commissary of the train, who will supply him with what he demands taking his, or his assistants receipts for the same.

The officers to provide themselves with bat horses as soon as possible.

The artillery to have their men upon the wharf every morning at 6 o'clock precisely to send their stores &c. and care must be taken that they have their waggons at the wharf exactly at the same time that there may be no delay one sergant and twelve men from the two regiments to march immediately to the wharf in order to assist the artillery in the landing of their stores this party to be relieved every morning and to be on the wharf precisely at 6 o'clock.

Sir Peter Halket's regiment receives three days' provisions tomorrow.

Camp at Alexandria, April 1st, 1755.
Parole—Esse.
Field officer for tomorrow ——
For the Generals Guard 48th Regiment. Colonel Dunbar's regiment to receive three days' provisions.

The two regiments are to send to artillery for one dozen of carts made up with ball in order to try if they will fit the men's firelocks.

Camp at Alexandria, April 2nd, 1755.
Parole—Farnham.
Field officer for tomorrow Major Chapman.
For the Generals Guard 44th Regiment.

The artillery and hospital receive three days' provision tomorrow.

The two regiments are to apply to the train for paper, powder and ball sufficient to compleat every man with twenty-four rounds which are to be made up, and distributed as soon as possible.

The commanding officers of companys are desired to give particular directions to their men to be careful of their ammunition and to inform them they will be very severly punished for any abuse or neglect of it, and the officers of companys who called the evening rolls are to inspect the ammunition of their several companys and to report the defficiencys to the commanding officers of the regiments who are desired by His Excellency to keep them compleat with twenty-four rounds.

His Excellency General Braddock orders that the soldiers should be told that any man who upon a march by fastning his tent pole, or by any other means incumbers his fire lock, shall be immediately and most severely punished.

One corporal and eight men of the line to attend at 6 o'clock every morning, to assist the engineers in surveying.

The artillery, hospital and engineers to receive three days' provisions tomorrow.

After Orders.

One sergeant one corporal, and twenty men of the line without arms to march to the wharf immediately to assist in disembarking the artillery.

The Virginia troops as appointed to the particular regiments.

140

Camp at Alexandria, April 3rd, 1755.

Parole—Canterbury.

Field officer tomorrow Lieutenant Colonel Burton. For the general's Guard 48th Regiment. The general's guard is this day reduced to a corporal and nine men and the corporal is to report to the officer of the main guard.

Sir Peter Halket's regiment to receive three days' provisions tomorrow.

Camp at Alexandria, 4th of April, 1755.

Parole—Dorsett.

Field officer tomorrow Major Sparke.

For the Generals Guard 44th Regiment.

Colonel Dunbar's regiment to have one corporal and six men ready to march tomorrow at 6 o'clock from Alexandria to Frederick with the hospital stores they are to carry six days' provisions with them and to take the arms and accoutrements with which they are to take the field Each man to have his blancket and twenty-nine rounds of ammunition.

Colonel Dunbar's regiment to have three days' provisions tomorrow.

Alexandria, Saturday, April 5th, 1755.

Parole—London .

Field officer tomorrow Lieutenant Colonel Burton.

For the general's Guard 48th Regiment.

The tents and clothing for the Virginia Company to be brought on shore as soon as possible; Their tents are to be pitched the first fair day after they are on shore.

The artillery hospital and engineers to receive three days' provisions tomorrow.

Alexandria, April 6th, 1755.

Parole—Kinsale.

Field officer for tomorrow Major Chapman.

For the general's Guard 44th Regiment.

All departments for duty of every nature whatever are to parade at the Grand Parade and to march from thence, detach-

141

ments from different corps to draw up by seniority.

The Grand Parade for this camp is appointed to be at the head of Sir Peter Halket's regiment.

A report to be made every morning to Sir Peter Halkets, of the sergeants, corporals, drummers and private men who are drunk upon duty, the sergeants of the companies they belong to, to keep an exact roll of their names, Sir Peter Halket being determined to put a stop to any more provisions being drawn for such men. Sergeants, corporals, drummers, and private men who appear drunk in camp though they are not upon duty will have their provisions stopped for one week.

Sir Peter Halket's regiment to receive three days' provisions tomorrow.

The detachments from the ordinary dutys of camp to change from right to left every day.

After Orders.

One sergeant, one corporal, and thirty men are tomorrow at 6 o'clock in the morning, to go to Alexandria to assist the officers of the artillery in loading the waggons for Winchester and shipping of stores for Rock Creek. One officer and thirty men from Colonel Dunbar's regiment to march tomorrow for Rock Creek The officer to call this night upon Sir Peter Halket who will give him his instructions.

Alexandria, Monday April 7th, 1755.
Parole—Dublin.
Field officer for tomorrow Lieutenant Colonel Burton.
For the General's Guard 48th Regiment.

One officer one sergeant and twenty men of Sir Peter Halket's regiment to hold themselves in readiness tomorrow morning to march to Winchester the officer at retreat beating to call upon Sir Peter Halket for his instructions; They are to take six days' provisions with them, subsistance to the 24th of this month and everything with which they are to take the field.

Every party ordered to march from camp is to have twenty-four rounds per man.

A greater number of women having been brought over than those allowed by the Government sufficient for washing with a view that the hospital might be served; and complaint being made that a concert is entered into not to serve without exorbitant wages a return will be called for of those who shall refuse to serve for six pence per day and their provisions that they may be turned out of camp and others got in their places.

Colonel Dunbar's regiment is to receive three days' provisions tomorrow.

Colonel Dunbar's regiment is to march at 5 o'clock on Saturday morning for Rock Creek.

Waggons will be ordered on Friday to carry the baggage and whatever tents may be struck to the boats destend for their transportation and at daybreak on Saturday morning Waggons will attend at the head of the regiment for the men's tents &c.

A subaltern officer with three sergeants, three corporals and thirty men are to be sent on board the boats as a baggage guard, and this guard is to assist in conveying the tents &c to the boats and to help in putting them on board.

All the boats upon that part of the river near Rock Creek are ordered to attend to cary the troop over.

The sick men that are not able to march with the regiment, to be left in the general hospital.

AFTER ORDERS.

As Colonel Dunbar's regiment is to march on Saturday, they are to receive tomorrow nine days' provisions one for tomorrows use and the remaining eight days the men are to carry with them.

The four companys of Sir Peter Halket's regiment, the Royal Regiment of Artillery engineers and the hospital are to continue to receive their provisions as usual till further orders.

March rout of Colonel Dunbar's regiment from the camp at Alexandria to Frederick in Maryland.

	Miles
To Rock Creek	—
To Owens Ordinary	15
To Dowden s Ordinary	15
To Frederick	15
	—
	45

Within a few miles of the Minocasy cross the Minocasy in a float.

Alexandria, Tuesday, April 8th, 1755.
Parole—Guilford.
Field Officer for tomorrow Major Sparke.
For the general's Guard 44th Regiment .

The quartermasters of Sir Peter Halket's and Colonel Dunbar's regiments to meet Mr. Leslie assistant quartermaster general this afternoon at 4 o'clock who will show them their regimental store houses.

The commanding officers of each of the regiments as soon as their regimental store houses are fixed are to order their officers baggage and their men's stores to be immediately lodged.

The soldiers are to leave their shoulder belts, waist belts and hangers behind and only to take with them to the field one spare shirt, one spare pair of stockings, one spare pair of shoes and one pair of brown gaters.

For the future the general's own and all other guards are to beat a march to him and the line is always to turn out when the general passes.

As a mistake has happened in regard to the commissions of the youngest subaltern of the rangers; The commissions of second lieutenant being delivered to them instead of ensigns are to be immediately changed to avoid any inconvenience, which may arise from disrules of rank.

His Excellency General Braddock orders that all ensigns bearing commissions in any of His Majesty's Regiments shall take post of the third officer in any of the companys of rangers.

After Orders.

Six companys of Sir Peter Halket's regiment are to march for Winchester at 6 o'clock on Thursday morning; Upon your arrival at Rock Creek you are either to encamp or lodge your men as you shall find most convenient and as fast as the waggons arrive you are to employ them in the service of ye regiment and regulate your detachments accordingly and to be particularly careful not to use any more waggons than are absolutely necessary.

You are to leave at Rock Creek an officer and thirty men who is to remain there till all the stores of the train and hospital are put into the waggons is then to march and form the rear guard of the whole.

You are also to leave at Rock Creek a subaltern and twenty men who are to wait there till the arrival of Mr. Johnston the paymaster and to escort him to Frederick.

You will .be joined at Rock Creek by an officer and thirty seamen who you are to take under your command and give them your orders and regulations as they will want some conveyance for their baggage you will dispose of it as you find most convenient.

Upon your arrival at Frederick you are to encamp your men the troops to remain there till further orders except a Captain D , two subalterns and fifty men who are to be sent immediately on to Conogogee as a covering party for the magazines and you are to direct the commanding officer of this detachment to stop all waggons which shall bring in flower, &c., from Pennsylvania and to send a daily to you of the numbers which return you are to remit to me unless you should see Sir John St. Clair and that he should have secured a sufficient number for transporting the stores from Frederick to Wills Creek in such case the waggons are to be dismissed.

You will find provisions at Frederick which you are to issue to your men in the same proportions as at Alexandria and to begin upon it as soon as you have expended the provisions card with you.

You are to direct your officers to provide themselves as soon as possible with bat horses as no more waggons will be allowed after they get to Frederick.

Alexandria, Wednesday, April 9th, 1755.
Parole—Henry.
Field officer for tomorrow Lieutenant Colonel Gage.
For the Generals Guard 48th Regiment.
Colonel Dunbar's regiment to send this forenoon two sergeants and twenty men to Rock Creek to reinforce the officer there.

A return to be given in this day of the two regiments specifying all extraordinarys that have happened since their embarking in Ireland a monthly return of the two regiments to be given in to General Braddock every first day of the month The companys of rangers artificers and the troop of light horse are to give in a monthly return at the same time: They are to apply to the major of brigade, who will shew them the proper form.

The officers to see that their men are provided as soon as possible with bladder or thin leather to put between the lining and crown of their hats to guard against the heat of the sun.

One subaltern officer of Dunbar's regiment to march tomorrow morning to Frederick in Mary land who upon his arrival is immediately to take upon him the command of the several detachments of the regiment that are now there or may arrive and he is to see yet they are properly provided and subsisted.

Alexandria, Thursday, 10th April, 1755.
Parole—Winchester.
A detachment from the two regiments of a subaltern, two sergeants, two corporals and twenty men is to remain at Alexandria as a guard for the hospital and to march with it to Frederick.

The General's Guard is to be taken off on Friday.

A sergeant and twelve men of Colonel Dunbar's regiment to mount as the general's baggage guard and to march with it.

The provost marshall is to march with Colonel Dunbar's regiment and to have a guard of a sergeant and ten men who is to make the rear of the whole.

Two officers and forty men of the four remaining companies of Sir Peter Halket's regiment is to mount the town guard till further orders.

Alexandria, Friday, April 11th, 1755.
Parole—Kendall.

The officer of the town guard to make his report to the general through an *aid de camp*.

AFTER ORDERS.

Colonel Dunbar's regiment to hold themselves in readiness but not to march till further orders.

They are to give their proportion of men for the Guard to-morrow; one sergeant, one corporal and twelve men to parade immediately at the town guard of Colonel Dunbar's regiment.

They are to take their knapsacks, haversacks, and provisions with them, when they come to the town guard the sergeant is to enquire for Mr. Leslie assistant quartermaster who will give him orders.

No person whatever to press or employ any waggons without an order from General Braddock the quartermaster general or his assistant.

This order to be read not only to the soldiers but to the officers, servants and followers of the army as anyone who shall be found guilty of disobeying it shall be severely punished.

AFTER ORDERS.

As there are boats provided to carry Colonel Dunbar's regiment's baggage to Rock Creek the former orders relative to their march to be obeyed.

Eight waggons will be ordered to be at the head of that regiment on Wednesday night for the tents, baggage, &c. of those companys' application is to be made to Mr Leslie assistant quartermaster for a proper guide; Every man is to receive eight days' provisions to carry with him. The lieutenant colonel is to be left with the eight remaining companys till farther orders.

All the sick are to be left in the general hospital.

The regiments find the General's Guard as usual and the proportion of duty is to be made up by Colonel Dunbar's regiment in the town and other guards.

March rout of Sir Peter Halket's regiment from the camp at Alexandria to Winchester.

	Miles
To ye old Court House	18
To Mr Coleman's on Sugar Land Run were there is Indian Corn, &c.	19
To Mr Miners	15
To Mr Thompson ye Quaker where ye is 3000 wt corn	12
To Mr They's 17 ye ferry of Shan'n 12	17
From Mr They's to Winchester	23
	—
	97

If the bridge should not be laid over the Opeckon canves will be provided for the troops.

As soon as the artillery arrives at Winchester a detachment of their regiment and whatever part you shall judge proper of the rangers must be ordered to march with the artillery to Wills Creek.

But if the road should be cut from the bridge on the Opeckon to Bear Garden and is made passable for ye artillery, It is then to go along that road and not by Winchester and your detachment from Winchester must join them at Henry Enochs ——, A report will be made to you whether this road is passable or not.

As the removal of the troops from Winchester to Wills Creek must depend upon the quantity of flower that is to be sent from Pennsylvania when a proper quantity is arrived you shall receive advice of it.

Alexandria, Saturday, April 12th, 1755.
Parole—Leicester.
One company of Sir Peter Halket's regiment to march to-

morrow morning, they are to parade opposite to the town guard at 6 o'clock where they will be joined by five waggons belonging to the artillery, which they are to take under their escort to Winchester.

The town guard to be reduced tomorrow morning to one subaltern officer and thirty men.

Mr Leslie will take care that there shall be at Sir Peter Halket's quarter guard this afternoon three waggons, one for the company's tents and baggage and the other two are to carry ye regiments spare arms and stores.

The men are to take eight days' provisions with them.

Alexandria, Sunday, April 13th, 1755.
 Parole—Marlborough.

Alexandria, Monday, April 14th, 1755.
Parole—Oxford .

Alexandria, Tuesday, April 15th, 1755.
Parole—Petersborough.

Alexandria, Wednesday, April 16th, 1755.
Parole—Rochester.

Thursday, April 17th, 1755.
Parole—Queen Town.

Friday, April 18th, 1755.
Parole—Salisbury.

Saturday, April 19th, 1755.
Parole—Tamworth .

The commanding officer of the artillery to apply to Mr. Leslie for a store house to lodge their new cloathing in, and the officers are to see that their men comply with the orders of the 8th of April (*viz*) to leave their shoulder belts, waist belts and hangers behind, and are only to take with them to the field one spare shirt one spare pair of stockings one spare pair of shoes and one pair of brown gaters.

Frederick, Monday, April 21st, 1755.
Parole—Dunbar.

Frederick, Tuesday, April 22nd, 1755.
Parole—Westminster.

One sergeant one corporal and twelve men to parade immediately at the town guard to march with the waggons laden with artillery stores to Conogogee and to return back with the waggons to Frederick as soon as they are unloaded.

Frederick. Wednesday, April 23rd, 1755.
Parole—Exeter.

The commanding officers of regiments to order their officers to provide themselves as soon as possible with bat men out of such recruits and levies, as are unfit to the duty to do the of soldier and such men are to be enlisted as can act as bat men and are to be taken for any term and to be alowed as effectives; and according to the number settled in Flanders three men to each company and four to the staff, you are to go immediately to that part of the Antietum that lies in the road to Connogogee arid press such boats or canoes as you shall meet with upon the river agreeable to the orders you shall receive from Governor Sharpe If you shall find any difficulty in the execution of this order, you are to send an express to me and you shall be immediately supplied with a party of men to inforce it sending word when they shall join you, and you are to collect all the boats &c. at that pass by the 28th of this month.

Frederick, Thursday, April 24th, 1755.
Parole—Yarmouth .

Frederick, Friday, April 25th, 1755.
Parole Appleby.

Colonel Dunbar's regiment to hold themselves in readiness to march by the 29th.

After Orders.

One corporal and four men to march tomorrow morning to Rock Creek with four waggons that came up this evening;

when the party comes to Rock Creek they are to put themselves under the command of Ensign French.

Frederick, Saturday, April 26th, 1755.
Parole—Bedford.
Colonel Dunbar's regiment to furnish three officers for a court martial, to try some prisoners of the Independant Company and Captain Gates President the report to be made to General Braddock.

Frederick, Sunday, April 27th, 1755
Parole—Chester.
Colonel Dunbar's regiment is to march ye 29th and to proceed to Wills Creek agreeable to the following route:

	Miles.
29th From Frederick on ye road to Conogogee	17
30th From that halting place to Congogee	18
1st From Conogogee to John Even's	16
2nd Rest	
3rd To the Widow Baringer	18
4th To George Polls	9
5th to Henry Enock's	15
6th Rest	
7th To Cox's at ye mouth of little Cacaph	12
8th To Colonel Cresap's	8
9th To Wills Creek	16
Total	129

The men are to take from this place three days' provisions; at Conogogee they will have more, at the Widow Baringer's five days, at Colonel Cresap's one or more days, and at all these places oats or Indian corn must be had for the horses but no hay.

At Conogogee the troops cross the Potomack in a float when the troops have marched fourteen miles from John Evans they are to make the new road to their right, which leads from Opeckon Bridge.

When the troops have marched fourteen miles from George Polls's they come to the great Cacapepon they are to pass that river in a float, after passing they take the road to the right.

If the water in the little Cacapepon is high the troops must encamp opposite to Cox's.

At the mouth of the little Cacapepon the Potomack is to be crossed in a float four miles beyond this they cross Town Creek if the float should not be finished canves will be provided.

If the bridges are not finished over Wills Creek and Evans Creek, waggons will be ordered to carry the men over. It will be proper to get two days' provisions at Colonel Cresap's ye whole slid not arrive till ye 10th.

A subaltern and thirty men are to be left behind with a proper number of tents which will be carried for them; these men are to have six days' provisions.

The General's Guard is not to be relieved tomorrow but proper centrys are to be found from the thirty men ordered to remain.

Frederick, Monday, April 28th, 1755.
Parole—Daventry.

The detachment of sailors, and the provost marshall's guard consisting of one sergeant, one corporal and ten men to march with Colonel Dunbar's regiment tomorrow morning, and to make the rear guard.

To Captain Gates, 28th April, 1755.

You are directed by His Excellency General Braddock to proceed with your company to Conogogee where you are to act as a covering party for the magazines, and you are to remain there till further orders unless all the stores, ammunition, &c., should be come up from Rock Creek and forwarded to Wills Creek, in that case you are to join the general at Wills Creek as soon as possible.

You are to give all possible assistance and use your utmost endeavours in transporting the several stores, ammunition, provision, &c. to Wills Creek with the utmost expedition.

Whilst you remain at Conogogee you are to send a sergant or corporal with such of your men as are to be trusted with all the waggon s which arrive at that place from Rock Creek allowing one man to each waggon and you are to send them immediately back to Rock Creek for more stores till you shall be informed from the officers there, that everything is sent up.

To Ensign French, at Rock Creek.
28th April, 1755.

You are ordered by his Excellency General Braddock to forward with all expedition the ammunition stores &c. at Rock Creek to Mr Cresap's Conogogee taking care to send the ammunition train stores &c. first, then the hospital stores and salt fish.

You are not wait for the Beeves but as soon as the aforementioned things are gone up you will move with your party and join the regiment at Wills Creek agreeable to the following march route; as you will find provisions very scarce on the road you must take with you as many days of salt provisions as the men can carry.

	Miles
From Rock creek to Owens Ordy	15
To Dowdens	15
To Frederick	15
On the road to Conogogee	17
To Conogogee	18
To John Evan's	16
To Widow Baringers	18
To George Polls's	9
To Henry Enocks	15
To Mr Cox's	12
To Colonel Cresap's	8
To Wills Creek	16
Total	174

You must if you should find it necessary, take with you guides from place to place, and make such halts as you shall find absolutely necessary being careful not to loose any time.

If the waggons should come in very slowly make your application to the civil officers and if that should not succeed send parties to fetch in any waggons you shall hear off. Inform Lieutenant Breerton of the march route, and tell him it is the General's Orders that he make all imaginable dispatch.

As soon as the paymaster arrives he must also victual his men when the last stores of all kinds which are to be sent and dismissed from Rock Creek, you are to send a letter to Captain Gates at Conogogee informing him of it.

The hand barrows and wheel barrows of the train except six of each are to be left behind all but the wheels and iron work which are to be forwarded.

Camp at Fort Cumberland,
Saturday, May 10th, 1755.
Parole—Connecticut.

Mr. Washington is appointed *aid de camp* to His Excellency General Braddock.

Field officer for tomorrow Major Sparke.

The articles of war to be read tomorrow morning, at which time the servants, women and followers of the army are to attend with the respective corps and companies that they belong to.

The two Independent companies and Rangers to receive three days' provisions tomorrow.

For the Generals Guard 48th Regiment.

Colonel Dunbar's regiment to relieve the fort guard immediately, and the fort guard is to march to Fraziers as a grass guard, and to be relieved every forty-eight hours. Captain Pilson's company of carpenters is to send one corporal and six men with their tools and to make such fences as the officer of the grass guard shall think proper.

The Virginia and Maryland Rangers and the company of carpenters to settle their men's accts immediately, giving them credit for what arrears &c. are due, and they are for the future to be subsisted regularly twice a week as the rest of troops are.

A return to be given in tomorrow morning of the strength of each of the regiments by companys, the return to be signed by the commanding officer of each corps the Independent Companys, Virginia and Maryland Rangers and the troop of light horse are also to send in a return tomorrow morning of their strength, which return is to be signed by the captain or officer commanding each company, and to be given in separately.

The general has fixed the hour for his levy, from ten till eleven in the forenoon every day.

Camp at Fort Cumberland.
Sunday, May 11, 1755.
Parole—Albany.

Field officer tomorrow Lieutenant Colonel Burton. The Generals Guard 44th Regiment.

A return to be sent in of the numbers of men who understand the springing of rocks. and those men that are fit are to be told that they will receive proper encouragement all the troops are to begin their field days. Powder may be had from the train by applying for it, and each man is to have twelve rounds for every field day.

A return is to be given in tomorrow morning at orderly time of the recruits of the whole army, setting forth their age size country and occupation one sargeant and six men from piquet to attend during the time of marketting to prevent disputes, and if any should happen he is to apply to the Captain of the picquet he belongs to. This duty to be done alternately.

All provisions brought into camp to be settled according to a settled rule, a copy of which will be given to the troops by the major of brigade and no person bringing provisions shall presume to ask more nor shall anybody offer less for good and wholesome meat.

The 48th Regiment is to receive their days provisions tomorrow at 10 o'clock.

After Orders.

All the out guards to be relieved tomorrow morn g and parade at 5 o clock.

It is His Excellency General Braddock's orders that no officer soldier or others give the Indians men women or children any rum other liquor or money upon any account whatever.

Camp at Fort Cumberland,
Monday, May 12th, 1755.
Parole—Boston.
Field officer tomorrow Major Sparke.
The Generals Guard 48th Regiment.

Whereas Captain Poulson, one of the Virginia company of carpenters desired a court martial to enquire into his character, having been accused of being in arms in the late rebellion in Scotland His Excellency has been informed that the accusations is scandalous and groundless; if therefore any person whatever can prove Captain Polson to have been in the late rebellion they are desired immediately to send their accusation to the general; if not his Excellency entirely frees him from any imputation of that kind, and desires that no reflections for the future may be thrown on Captain Polson on that account.

After Orders.

A general court martial to sit immediately at the President's tent, it is to consist of one field officer, six captains and six subalterns.

Major Sparke President.
Mr Shirley Judge Advocate.

His Excellency has thought proper to brigade the army in the following manner and they are for the future to encamp accordingly:

The first Brigade, Commanded by Sir Peter Halket.

	Compliment.	Effective
44th Regiment of Foot	700	700
Captain Rutherford's Captain Gates		

Independant Company of New York	100	95
Captain Polson's Carpenters	50	48
Captain Peronnee's Virginia Rangers	50	47
Captain Wagner's Virginia Rangers	50	45
Captain Dagworthy's Maryland Rangers	50	49

Second Brigade, Commanded by Colonel Dunbar

48th Regiment of Foot	700	650
Captain Demerie's Sth Carol. Detach	100	97
Captain Dobb's Nth Carol. Rangers	100	80
Captain Mercer's Coy of Carpenters	50	35
Captain Stevens Virginia Rangers	50	48
Captain Hogg's Virginia Rangers	50	40
Captain Cox's Virginia Rangers	50	43

Any soldier or follower of the army who shall stop any one bringing in provisions or forage to the camp shall immediately suffer death.

No outpost to march from or to camp with beat of drum, nor is any beat of drum to beat before the troop unless when any of the troops are out at exercise, and of which they are to acquaint the general the night before through one of his *aid de camps.*

Camp at Fort Cumberland,
Tuesday, 13th May, 1755.
Parole—Charleston.
Field Officer for tomorrow Lieutenant Colonel Burton.
For the Generals Guard 44th Regiment.

The quartermasters, camp colour men, and pioneers of the two regiments with two men of the Independent Companies with proper tools for clearing the ground in the front to parade at five o'clock in the evening at the head of the 48th Regiment, and to remain there for the field officer of the day's orders.

The picquetts are to lay advanced and to remain at their parade till they receive the field officers orders. Each of the two regiments to send six tents to the companies in each brigade, and also to send six tents each for the men of their advanced picquets. The centrys on the advanced picquetts not to suffer any body to pass unquestioned after sun set.

The picquett returns at 6 o'clock in the morning.

The quarter guard of Sir Peter Halket's regiment for the future to be posted on the right flank.

Camp at Fort Cumberland,
Wednesday, 14th May. 1755.
Parole—Dumfries.
Field Officer tomorrow Lieutenant Colonel Burton.
The Generals Guard 48th Regiment.

The General Court Martial is dissolved. Luke Woodward soldier in the 48th Regiment, commanded by Colonel Dunbar. having been tryed for desertion by a general court martial whereof Major William Sparke was president, is by sentence of that general court martial adjudged to suffer death. His Excellency General Braddock has approved of the sentence, but has been pleased to pardon him.

Thomas Conelly, James Fitzgerald and James Hughes, soldiers in the 48th Regiment, and tryed for theft by the said Court Martial whereof Major Sparke was President, are by the sentence of the said court martial adjudged to suffer the following punishments:

Thomas Conelly one thousand, Jas Fitzgerald, eight hundred, Jas Hughes eight hundred lashes of the line.

Also that they be obliged to make satisfaction for the kegg of beer stolen by them to the value of thirty three shillings Maryland Cur'y, and that proper stopages be made out of their pay by their officers for that purpose; His Excellency has approved the sentence, but has been pleased to remit one hundred lashes from the punishment of Conelly and two hundred from each of the other two. Conelly is to receive 900 lashes at three different times 300 lashes each time. Jas Fitzgerald and Jas Hughes are to receive 600 lashes each at two different times, 300 lashes each time. The 48th Regiment to send the drummers to the head of ye line, to put the sentence in execution, the first time of punishment to be tomorrow morning at troop beating. The two picquetts formed from the Independent Companies Virginia and Maryland Rangers, to consist of one Captain, two subalterns, two sergeants, two corporals and thirty-eight centinals.

Camp at Fort Cumberland,
Thursday, 15th May, 1755.
Parole—Portsmouth.
Field Officer tomorrow Major Sparke.
For the Generals Guard 44th Regiment.

The officers who were ordered to get themselves in readiness to go with the paymaster are continued.

On subaltern, one sergeant one corporal and thirty centinels to march this evening to Mr Martin's where the troop of light horse graze, the men to take tents with them and provisions for three days, the officer to receive his orders from Captain Stuart of the light horse; this guard to be relieved every 3rd day.

One sergeant one corporal and twelve men to parade at the fort guard this day at 12 o'clock m.

The sergeant will receive his orders from Captain Orme.

AFTER ORDERS.

The subalterns guard that was ordered to march to Martin's is countermanded.

Camp at Fort Cumberland,
Friday, 16th May, 1755.
Parole Winchester.
Field officer tomorrow Lieutenant Colonel Gage.
For the Generals Guard 44th Regiment.

Any Indian trader, soldier or follower of the army who shall dare to give liquor to any of the Indians or shall receive or purchase from them any of their presents made to them by His Majesty through His Excellency General Braddock, shall suffer the severest punishment a court martial can inflict.

There will be a public congress of the Indians tomorrow at 12 o clock at the general's tent.

Camp at Fort Cumberland,
Saturday, 17th of May, 1755.
Parole—Eskaw.

The congress of Indians mentioned in yesterdays orders is put off.

Field officer tomorrow Lieutenant Colonel Burton. For the Generals Guard 48th Regiment.

The two regiments, the Independent companys, the companys of carpenters, the Virginia and Maryland company of Rangers and the troop of light horse are to send immediately to Mr Lake, commissary of Provisions a separate return of the number of persons they each of them draw provisions for, this return to be signed by the commander of the two regiments and by the Captains or officers commanding each of the independent companys &c. The form of this return is sent to the brigade major and is to be given in regularly every eight days.

His Excellency expects that this order will be punctually obeyed, as the commissary will not be able to provide a proper quantity of provisions for the army unless he has the above return sent to him regularly.

One subaltern, one sergeant one corporal, and thirty men to mount as a guard on the artillery, They are to parade this afternoon at 5 o'clock and to be relieved every forty-eight hours.

Camp at Fort Cumberland,
Sunday, May 18th, 1755.
Parole—Farnham.

There will be a public congress of the Indians this day at 12 o'clock at the general's tent.

Field officer tomorrow Major Sparke.

For the Generals Guard 44th Regiment.

One corporal, and eight men of the line to attend the engineer in surveying; they are to parade at 9 o'clock.

Each regiment, Independent Company &c. in the making up of their cartridges are to allow thirty-six round of ball to 1 lb of powder, and for field days or exercise they are to allow forty-six with or without ball.

Six women per company are allowed to each of the two regiments and the Independent companys; Four women to each of the companys of carpenters Virginia and Maryland Rangers five women to the troop of light horse, as many to the detachment of seamen, and five to the detachment of artillery.

His Excellency expects that this order will be punctually complied with, as no more provision will be allowed to be drawn for than for the above number of women.

Camp at Fort Cumberland,
Monday, 19th of May, 1755.
Parole—Guilford.
Field officer tomorrow Lieutenant Colonel Gage.
For the Generals Guard 44th Regiment.

Each brigade to send a man to the general hospital as orderly who are to recieve and obey the directions of Doctor Napper Director of the 2nd hospital.

All the troops are to act with the director of the hospital once in three months or as soon after as can be, for stoppages at the rate of five pence sterling per day, for every man that is admitted in the general hospital; this stoppage to commence from the 24th of May ensuing.

As soon as the retreat has been beat this night the drum major of each of the two regiments are to march with the drummers and drummers to the head of the artillery where they will receive orders.

A return to be given into the brigade major tomorrow at orderly time of the number of smiths and carpenters that are in the two regiments, Independent Companies &c.

Camp at Fort Cumberland.
Tuesday, May the 20th, 1755.
Parole—Hendon.
Field officer tomorrow Lieutenant Colonel Burton.
For the Generals Guard 48th Regiment.

One subaltern, one sergeant, one corporal and twenty-four men to parade tomorrow morning at 5 o'clock They are to have three days' provisions with them and the officer is this night to recieve his orders from Sir John St. Clair.

Camp at Fort Cumberland.
Wednesday, 21st of May 1755.
Parole—Ilchester.
 Field officer tomorrow Major Chapman.
The Generals Guard 44th Regiment.

No soldier that is employed as a baker by Mr Lake, commissary of provisions, is to be put upon any duty whatever till further orders.

It is His Excellency's orders that no sutler give any liquor to the Indians on any account: if any one does he will be severely punished.

The provost is to go his round every day through all the roads leading to the camp. Every soldier or woman that he shall meet with on the other side of the river, or beyond the advanced picquets without a pass from the regiment or from the officer commanding the company to which they belong, he is to order his executioner to tye them up and give them fifty lashes and to march them prisoners through the camp to expose them.

One gill of spirits mixed with three gills of water may be allowed each man per day, which the officers of the picquet are to see delivered out every day at eleven o'clock, any settler that shall sell any spirits to the soldiers without an officer being present shall be sent to the provosts.

Camp at Fort Cumberland,
Tuesday, 22nd May, 1755.
Parole—Kensington,
Field officer tomorrow Major Sparke.
The Generals Guard 48th Regiment.

Camp at Fort Cumberland,
Friday, May 23rd, 1755.
Parole—Lincoln.
Field officer tomorrow Major Chapman.
For the Generals Guard 44th Regiment.

A general court martial to sit tomorrow morning, at 8 o'clock at the general's tent to consist of one field officer, six captains six subalterns.

Lieutenant Colonel Gage President.

Mr Shirley Judge Advocate.

If any officer, soldier or follower of the army shall dare to give any strong liquor, or money to the Indian men or women, if an officer he shall be brought to a general court martial for disobedience of orders; if a non commissioned officer soldier or follower of the army he shall receive 250 lashes without a court martial.

Camp at Fort Cumberland,
Saturday, 24th May, 1755.
Parole—Monmouth.
Field officer tomorrow Lieutenant Colonel Burton.
For the Generals Guard 48th Regiment.

Camp at Fort Cumberland,
Sunday, May 25th, 1755.
Parole—Norwich.
Field officer tomorrow Major Sparke.
For the Generals Guard 44th Regiment.

If any non commissioned officer or soldier belonging to the army is found gaming he shall immediately receive three hundred lashes without being brought to court martial, and all slanders by or lookers on shall be deemed principals and punished as such.

One captain, one lieutenant, one ensign and seventy men of the two brigades to parade immediately at the fort. They are to take tents and ten days' provisions with them. The captain is to receive his orders from Sir John St Clair.

A general court martial of the line, to sit tomorrow to try Lieutenant McLead of the Royal Regiment of Artillery confined by General Braddock to consist of one colonel two field officers, and ten captains.

Sir Peter Halket President.

Mr Shirley Judge Advocate.

To sit at the President's tent and to meet at 12 o'clock.

Camp at Fort Cumberland,
Monday, 26th May, 1755
Parole—Oxford.
Field Officer tomorrow Lieutenant Colonel Gage.
For the Generals Guard 48th Regiment.

The general court martial whereof Lieutenant Colonel Gage was President is dissolved His Excellency having approved of the several sentences allotted them.

John Nugent of the 44th Regiment having been tryed for theft and found guilty of the crime laid to his charge as an accomplice in receiving a share of the money that was stole, is adjudged to receive one thousand lashes, and to be drummed out of the regiment through the line with a halter about his neck.

Samuel Draumer, of the 44th Regiment and George Darty of Captain Demere's Independent Company having been tryed for desertion are adjudged each of them to receive two hundred lashes.

Henry Dalton, of the 48th Regiment having been tryed for shooting Henry Pelkington, soldier in the said regiment the court marshal is of opinion that the said Dalton did not shoot the said Pelkington with design but that it was done by accident, therefore His Excellency General Braddock has ordered him to be released and to be sent back to his duty.

If any soldier is seen drunk in camp he is to be sent immediately to the quarter guard of the regiment he belongs to, and the next morning he is to receive two hundred lashes without a court martial.

Camp at Fort Cumberland,
Tuesday, May 2 7th, 1755.
Parole—Petersfield.
Field officer tomorrow Lieutenant Colonel Burton.
For the Generals Guard 44th Regiment.
The party of the picquets that lay advanced to load with rain-

ing ball, the rest of the picquets to load with powder and to have their ball in their pockets.

The following detachments to march on Tuesday morning to parade at revelle beating The men to be provided with two days provisions ready dressed. The 44th, 48th Regiments are to furnish one field officer, four captains twelve subalterns twelve sergeants and 250 rank and file.

Captain Rutherford's Captain Demere's Independent Companys, Captain Waginer's Captain Peyrouney's Companies of Virginia Rangers and Captain Polson's Company of Carpenters are also to march with this detachment, who are to take with them their camp equippage and baggage.

Major Chapman field officer for the detachment.

The Independent Company and companys of Virginia Rangers ordered for this detachment to furnish no men for the guards tomorrow and any men that they may have upon the out guards are to be relieved immediately. Particular care is to be taken that the men s arms are in good order and that each man is provided with ten flints and compleated to twenty-four rounds of ammunition.

The tools and tomahawks of the 2nd Brigade are to be given at gun firing this evening to the quarter master general at his tent and a demand to be made tomorrow night at 6 o'clock of ye number of tools each brigade will want, the quarter master to attend.

Camp at Cumberland,
Wednesday, May 28th, 1755.
Parole—Quarendon.
Field officer tomorrow Major Sparke.
Generals Guard 48th Regiment.

The regulation of stoppages with the director of the general hospital to commence from the 24th of this month.

As it is necessary to employ the soldiers in making and amending the roads His Excellency has been pleased to appoint the following allowances

	(Sterling per day) s	d
To every sub: officer	3	0
To every sergeant	1	0
To every corporal	0	9
To every drummer and private centinal	0	6

But as at present there is no public market and of course the men will have no opportunity of making use of the ready money His Excellency is so kind as to promise that he will see that they are punctually paid whatever is due to them when they arrive in winter quarters therefore whatever Subaltern officer or sergeant has the command of any working party as soon as they are relieved or come back they are to make an exact return of the number of men of their party and give it in to the quarter master general.

But if hereafter there should be any public market or that the money will be found to be of use to the men upon a proper application His Excellency will give orders for their being paid.

The companies of Rangers are for the future to furnish their proportion of men for duty with the rest of the line.

As there will be an express going in a few days, any officers that have any letters to send to Great Britain are desired to give them to either the general's *aid de camps* or to Mr. Shirley.

After Orders.

The men of the detachment that march tomorrow to be commanded by the officers of their own corps or company.

Sixteen men from line to be appointed to the guns tomorrow that march and to be under the direction of the officer of artillery.

The Independant company and Rangers of the two brigades to mount but one picquet.

Camp at Fort Cumberland,
Thursday, 29th May, 1755.
Parole—Queensbury.
Field officer tomorrow Lieutenant Colonel Gage.

The Generals Guard 44th Regiment.

Camp at Fort Cumberland,
Friday, 30th of May, 1755.
Parole—Rochester.
Field officer tomorrow Lieutenant Colonel Burton.
Generals Guard 48th Regiment.

The troops to hold themselves in readiness to march in twenty-four hours warning.

Whatever barrells the regiments and companys have got belonging to the artillery are to be sent back immediately with their troops to the foreman of the train.

Camp at Fort Cumberland,
Saturday, 31st May, 1755.
Parole ——
Field Officer tomorrow Major Sparke.
Generals Guard 44th Regiment.

Camp at Fort Cumberland,
Sunday, 1st of June, 1755,
Parole—Tamworth .
Field officer tomorrow Lieutenant Colonel Gage.
Generals Guard 48th Regiment.

Camp at Fort Cumberland,
Monday, 2nd of June, 1755.
Parole Weybridge.
Field officer tomorrow Lieutenant Colonel Burton.
Generals Guard 44th Regiment.

The hatchet men of the two regiments and one man per company from the rest of the line to parade this afternoon at 3 o'clock at Mr Gordon's (engineer) tent.

Four sergeants two corporals and 100 men with arms one subaltern, one sergeant one corporal and thirty men with arms to parade tomorrow morning at revelle beating at the head of the line and to receive their orders from Mr Gordon engineer.

His Excellency has been pleased to appoint Colonel Innes

Governor of Fort Cumberland.

Monday evening.

Three subaltern officers to march with the detachment of 100 men without arms, which is to parade tomorrow morning at revelle beating.

Camp at Fort Cumberland.
Tuesday, June 3rd, 1755.
Parole—Yarmouth

A general court martial of the line consisting of six captains and six subalterns to sit tomorrow morning at 8 o'clock at the Presidents tent.

Major Sparke President.

Mr Shirley Judge Advocate.

Field officer tomorrow Lieutenant Colonel Burton.

Generals Guard 48th Regiment.

Four subalterns, five sergeants, five corporals, and 150 men without arms to parade tomorrow morning at ye head of the line at revelle beating.

One subaltern, one sergeant, one corporal, and thirty men with arms to parade at the same time and act as a covering party; they are to receive their order from Mr Gordon, engineer.

Camp at Fort Cumberland,
Wednesday, 4th June, 1755.
Parole—Doncaster.

Field officer tomorrow Lieutenant Colonel Burton.

For the Generals Guard 44th Regiment.

The 44th Regiment and Captain Mercer's Company of Virginia Carpenters to hold themselves in readiness to march in an hour s warning. The working party to be relieved tomorrow morning, and by the same number.

Camp at Fort Cumberland,
Thursday, June 5th, 1755.
Parole—Boston.

Field officer tomorrow Major Sparke.

For the Generals Guard 48th Regiment.

The working party to be relieved tomorrow morning and by the same number of men.

Camp at Fort Cumberland,
Friday, June 6th, 1755.
Parole ——

Field officer tomorrow Lieutenant Colonel Burton.

Sir Peter Halket's regiment to march tomorrow morning; the sick of the regiment unable to march to be sent to the general hospital. One subaltern officer to be left behind with them.

The men of Sir Peter Halket's regiment now upon guard when they are relieved or ordered to come off are to be assembled together and marched regularly to the regiment by an officer.

Captain Gates s Independant Company and all ye remaining companies of provincial troops to march on Sunday morning with the whole park of artillery.

No more women are allowed to march with each regiment and company than the number allowed of by His Excellency in the orders of the 18th of May.

Any soldier, sutler, woman or other person whatever who shall be detected in stealing, purloining or wasting of any provisions shall suffer death.

The general court martial whereof Major Sparkes was President is dissolved.

Michael Shelton and Caleb Sary, soldiers belonging to Captain Edward Brice Dobbs's company of Americans tryed for desertion are by sentence of the court martial found guilty and adjudged to receive 1,000 lashes each.

John Igo, a convict servant, accused of theft is by the sentence of the court martial found guilty of receiving and concealing goods the property of soldiers in His Majesty s service and is adjudged to receive 500 lashes with a cat and nine tails by the hands of the common hangman.

John McDonald soldier in Sir Peter Halket's regiment accused of being an accomplice and concerned with John Igo is acquitted.

The Guards advanced up Wills Creek, the Potomac and the Flats [1] to be taken off tomorrow morning, and to join their several corps, the other guards to remain and to he relieved as usual.

Captain Gates Independent Company and ye remaining companies of the Provincial Troops to furnish their proportion for the Guards tomorrow and when they are relieved they are to join their companys in the same manner as those of Sir Peter Halket's regiment are directed to do in this days orders.

No soldier's wife to be suffered to march from this ground with a horse as their own.

Camp at Fort Cumberland,
Saturday, June 7th, 1755.
Parole—Doncaster.

Captain Yates's Independant Companies and the remaining companies of Provincial Troops and ye whole park of artillery to march tomorrow morning and to be under the command of Lieutenant Colonel Burton.

The artillery and companies that march tomorrow to receive this afternoon provisions to compleat them to the 11th inclusive and ye women to ye 17th.

The 48th Regiment to take all the Guards tomorrow; the men of the 48th Regiment now upon ye train Guard are to join their corps tomorrow morning when the artillery marches off and that Guard to be mounted by the companys that march tomorrow.

The 48th Regiment to hold themselves in readiness to march on Monday next.

AFTER ORDERS.

The Generals Guard is to be reduced tomorrow to one sergeant one corporal and twelve men who are not to be relieved but to remain with the general's baggage.

---

1. The Flats were on the East side of Wills Creek.

Camp at Fort Cumberland,
Sunday, June 8th, 1755.
Parole—Essex.

Captain Gates's Independant Company and the remaining companys of the provincial troops and artillery are to march tomorrow.

The 48th Regiment to march on Tuesday as Colonel Dunbar's regiment is not to march tomorrow the Generals Guard to be relieved tomorrow morning.

The companies that march tomorrow to send immediately one sergeant corporal and twelve men to assist Mr Lake commissary of provisions at the fort.

A return to be sent immediately from Colonel Dunbar's regiment Captain Gates's company and the American troops of the number of men they have fit for waggoners or horse drivers.

In the return of Colonel Dunbar's regiment they are only to include those men that have joined the regiment since they have been landed in America.

Camp in Fort Cumberland,
Monday, June 9th, 1755.
Parole—Fallmouth.

Colonel Dunbar's regiment to send their sick unable to march to the general hospital and to leave a subaltern officer behind with them.

One sergeant, one corporal and twenty-four men without arms to parade tomorrow morning at daybreak to assist Mr Lake, commissary of provisions in loading of ye waggons.

Camp at Fort Cumberland,
Tuesday, June the 10th, 1755.

The fort guard to join their regiments as soon as Governor Innes has taken possession of it and placed his centrys.

Camp at the Grove,
(First Camp from Fort Cumberland.)
Parole—Gainsborough.

All the officers of the line to be at the general's tent tomorrow morning at 11 o'clock.

No fires to be made upon any account whatever within 150 yards of the road on either side, any person acting contrary to this order shall be very severely punished.

All the waggons to be drawn up tomorrow morning as close as possible and as soon as the waggons belong to the detachment under the command of Major Chapman have closed up to the rear of the artillery that detachment then to join the respective corps.

Colonel Dunbar's regiment to encamp tomorrow morning upon the left of the whole, according to the line of encampment.

Camp at the Grove,
Wednesday. June 11th, 1755.
Parole—Hartford .

Captain Rutherford and Captain Gates Independent companys and all the American's troops to be under arms immediately at the head of their respective encampments.

Any person whatsoever that is detected in stealing shall be immediately hanged without being brought to a court martial.

One subaltern officer one sergeant one corporal and forty men without arms from each of ye two regiments to parade immediately at ye head of the artillery.

One subaltern one sergeant one doctor and thirty men of the line to parade in the rear of Colonel Dunbar's regiment as soon as they have come to their proper ground The officer is to receive his orders from Major Sparkes.

Whatever number of horses are furnished by the officers are to be paraded as soon as possible in the rear of Colonel Dunbar's regiment and to be reviewed by Major Sparkes.

The officers are desired to acquaint Major Sparkes which of their horses for carrying horses and which are for draught and to be so good as to send with the carrying horses, bat-saddles and etc. if they have them.

The commanding officers of the two regiments and the captains of the Independent and Provencial troops to send in a return to the general of the number of horses furnished by their respective officers, and opposite to the officer s names, The number of horses furnished by each officer; that the general may be able to inform His Majesty of the inclination and readiness of the particular officers in carrying on the service.

AFTER ORDERS.

No more than two women per company to be allowed to march from the camp, a list of the names of those that are to be sent back to be given into Captain Morris that there may be an order sent to Colonel Innes at Fort Cumberland to victual them.

A list of the names of the women that are allowed to stay with the troops to be given into the major of brigade and any woman that is found in camp and whose name is not in that list will for the first time be severely punished and for the second suffer death.

AFTER ORDERS.

Colonel Dunbar's regiment is immediately to furnish a sergeant and twelve men as a guard for the provisions on their left and the sergeant is to receive his orders from M Lake Company of Provisions.

The line is to furnish two sergeants and thirty men without arms who are to attend Mr Lake Company of provisions tomorrow morning at daybreak and assist in loading the horses.

It is the general orders yet Mr Lake Company of provisions with his people and ye party yet is allowed him begin weighing out ye flour and other provisions for back two days tomorrow morning by daybreak and his Excellency yet everything will be in readiness by 1 o'clock in ye afternoon.

General Braddock's Orderly Book, No. 2.

Camp at the Grove,
Thursday, June 12th, 1755.
Parole—"Ilford."
Field officer of the picquet Lieutenant Colonel Gage.

The picquet to load with cartridges, and not with raming ball, to challenge and demand the counter sign till troop beating; and the field officer and picquet to be always received as grand rounds as often as he thinks proper to visit the out posts, by night or day.

The advanced corporals and sentrys to have their bayonets fixed; the detached partys from the sergeants' guard to have corporals with them; the advanced sentrys not to suffer anybody to come within ten paces of their arms without demanding the countersign.

The advanced partys not to build any bowers, upon pain of severest punishment; those already built to be immediately destroyed.

These orders to be read to the men, by the officer of ye picquet before the out guards are posted.

Whatever communications from sergeants' guards to sergeants' guards, and from corporals' guards to corporals' guards are not yet opened to be done immediately. This to be a standing order, and to be observed by ye troops in all camps, and no person whatever to fire their arms within a mile of ye camp, but in case of an alarm or their being attacked.

These orders to be read to the men by the commanding officer of each company, and the orders relative to the men of the picquet to be read to them before they are detached on ye out guards by the officers of ye picquet.

The captains of ye several picquetts to be at ye field officer of ye picquet's tent an hour before retreat beating in order to receive the countersign from him.

All the troops to be compleated this afternoon with provisions to the 16th inclusive and the waggon and horse drivers to the 26th.

AFTER ORDERS.

Sir Peter Halket's grenadiers and the battalion company s of that regiment to march immediately to the crossing of the new and old road, a little beyond where the detachment of seamen are now encamped. They are to encamp there; the grenadiers camp across the road and the battalion companys according to the present line of encampment covering the advanced wagons. The commanding officers to take care to advance picquets in the same manner and proportion of numbers as ordered in the disposition of march and to take care that his advanced picquets comply with the orders of this day.

The detachment of seamen commanded by Mr Spendelow to be disposed of in such parts of the line as he shall think proper, and their arms and accoutrements are to be carried in whatever waggons he shall appoint.

Three hatchet men of ye line with their tools to remain constantly with the detachment of seamen, and to receive their orders from Mr Spendelowe.

One tumbril with tools to march in the front immediately after Captain Polson's company of carpenters and another tumbril of tools to march in the centre of the carriages.

One engineer to march with Captain Polson's company of carpenters and another engineer is to march in the centre of ye carriages.

The pioneers of every company of ye line with their tools (except those that are ordered to ye detachment of seamen) to march constantly in ye centre of ye carriages and to be under the directions ye engineer who marches in the centre.

The troops to march tomorrow and the general to beat at four o clock in ye morning.

Camp at ——Friday, 13th June, 1755.
Parole—"Hertford."
Field officer tomorrow Major Chapman.
The line is not to march tomorrow.

Camp at Martin's, Saturday, June 14, 1755.
Parole—"Leicester."
Field officer tomorrow Lieutenant Colonel Burton.

Upon the beating of the general which is to be taken from Sir Peter Halket's regiment, all ye troops are to accoutre turn out and form two deep at ye head of their respective encampments, and there wait for further orders and no soldiers tent to be suffered to be struck till ordered by the general.

As soon as the tents are struck they are to be immediately loaded as also the officers' baggage and then the troops are to lay upon their arms till they recieve an order to inarch and upon the beating of ye march the whole to face to the right and left.

The field officers are not to be particularly posted excepting the one who marches at ye head of ye vanguard.

The number of carriages to be equally divided and Sir Peter Halket and his field officers with the troops of his brigade are to take under their care half of carriages and see that their officers order their men to assist the waggoners upon any point or difficulty that may happen.

Colonel Dunbar and his field officers with ye troops of the second brigade to act in the same manner with the remaining number of carriages.

In case any wagon should break down in such a manner as to be unable to keep with the line it is immediately to be drawn out on one side of the road and a report of it with what it is loaded to be sent to Mr Scott Wagon master general who is to order it to be repaired, or see that the load is divided among the rest of the wagons as he shall think proper.

Upon any halt, though ever so small the companys are to form two deep and face outward.

Upon a march the captains and officers of ye picquet to visit frequently their out detachments, and sec that they keep at a proper distance from their companies.

Upon ye firing of a cannon either in ye front, centre or rear the whole line to form face outwards and then wait for further orders.

When the troops come to Savage River the servants, bat men waggoners and horse drivers must take particular care to prevent their horses from eating of laurel, as it is certain death to them The general to beat tomorrow morning at 4 o clock.

AFTER ORDERS.

Upon the beating of the general tomorrow morning two companys from the right of Sir Peter Halket's regiment to strike their tents and march as an escort to the carrying horses of ye army The commanding officer to apply to Captain Morris tomorrow morning for his orders.

[Here is an omission of two days orders, which cannot be supplied, but a blank may be left in the records to show the chasm.][1]

Camp at the Little Meadows,
Tuesday, June 17th, 1755.
Parole—Orford.

Field officer tomorrow Lieutenant Colonel Burton. A detachment to march tomorrow morning at 4 o clock consisting of one field officer two captains six subalterns twelve sergeants and 150 rank and file of ye two regiments; Captain Gates two subalterns two sergeants two corporals and fifty private men of his independent company, Captain Waggoner's and Captain Per-

---

1. This note is written in Washington's handwriting.

ouney's companys of Rangers.

Lieutenant Colonel Gage to command this detachment. A detachment to march on Thursday morning at 4 o'clock consisting of one colonel one lieutenant colonel one major the two oldest companys of grenadiers five captains twenty subalterns twenty-two sergeants and 550 rank and file of ye two regiments.

Sir Peter Halket Lieutenant Colonel Burton and Major Sparke field officers for this detachment The King's colour of ye 44th Regiment and ye second colour of ye 48th Regiment to be sent with this detachment.

The men of the two regiments that are to march with the detachment of tomorrow and Thursday to be taken out of those which landed from Ireland the commanding officer of each regiment to be answerable to his Excellency that this is complied with.

A return to be sent in tomorrow morning to either of ye *aids de camp* signed by the commanding officers of ye companys of ye two regiments of ye names and countries of ye men that are for ye above two detachments their term of service and the regiments they have served in.

His Excellency has been pleased to appoint the following captains and subalterns officers for ye above detachments and desires that they will take with them as little baggage as possible.

For ye detachment and command of Lieutenant Colonel Gage.

Of ye 44th Regiment	Of ye 48th Regiment
Captain Beckwith	Captain Morris
Lieutenant Treby	Lieutenant Harsard
Lieutenant Sittler	Lieutenant Barbutt
Ensign Clarke	Ensign Dunbar

For the detachment that marches on Thursday.

Of the 44th Regiment	Of the 48th Regiment
Captain Hobson	Captain Dobson
Gethius	Cholmley

	Bowyer
Lieutenant Halkett	Lieutenant Walsam
Bailey	Hathorn
Pottinger	Edmonstone
Simpson	Cope
Lock	Brierton
Kennedy	Hurt
Townshend	Gladwin
Ensign Nortlow	Ensign Cowart
Pennington	Harrison
Preston	Crowe
	McMullen.

The surgeons mate of ye 48th Regiment to march with this detachment.

Captain Rutherford's Independent Company and Captain Stephen's company of Rangers, to march tomorrow morning with the detachment under ye command of Lieutenant Colonel Gage and to return to camp at night.

One corporal and four light horse to march tomorrow morning with the detachment under Colonel Gage's command, and to remain with him.

The detachment of seamen and Captain Stuart with one subaltern, and eighteen light horse to march on Thursday morning.

No woman to be victualled upon the detachments that march tomorrow and Thursday.

AFTER ORDERS

Each of the two regiments as also Captain Gate's Independent Company to send a sufficient number of tents for ye respective detachments that march tomorrow under ye command of Lieutenant Colonel Gage.

AFTER ORDERS

His Excellency has been pleased to appoint Lieutenant Buchanan of ye artillery to march with ye two guns tomorrow morning and Captain L Smith and Lieutenant McLoud of ye artillery to march with ye detachment on Thursday morning. The men that march tomorrow and on Thursday morning to be compleated to twenty-four rounds of ammunition.

[2]N. B.— After the orders in this, and the book preceding it, are transcribed, leave six pages blank for insertion of the commission of G. W——n and the proceedings which intervened between the defeat of General Braddock and the resumption of the command by G. W.

Next, the letters, instructions, and orders, in the order they appear in the parchment covered book, are to be transcribed.

---

2. The above appears in Washington's handwriting, on a page following the last of the recorded orders.

LEONAUR

ALSO FROM LEONAUR
AVAILABLE IN SOFTCOVER OR HARDCOVER WITH DUST JACKET

CAPTAIN OF THE 95th (Rifles) *by Jonathan Leach*—An officer of Wellington's Sharpshooters during the Peninsular, South of France and Waterloo Campaigns of the Napoleonic Wars.

BUGLER AND OFFICER OF THE RIFLES *by William Green & Harry Smith* With the 95th (Rifles) during the Peninsular & Waterloo Campaigns of the Napoleonic Wars

BAYONETS, BUGLES AND BONNETS *by James 'Thomas' Todd*—Experiences of hard soldiering with the 71st Foot - the Highland Light Infantry - through many battles of the Napoleonic wars including the Peninsular & Waterloo Campaigns

THE ADVENTURES OF A LIGHT DRAGOON *by George Farmer & G.R. Gleig*—A cavalryman during the Peninsular & Waterloo Campaigns, in captivity & at the siege of Bhurtpore, India

THE COMPLEAT RIFLEMAN HARRIS *by Benjamin Harris as told to & transcribed by Captain Henry Curling*—The adventures of a soldier of the 95th (Rifles) during the Peninsular Campaign of the Napoleonic Wars

WITH WELLINGTON'S LIGHT CAVALRY *by William Tomkinson*—The Experiences of an officer of the 16th Light Dragoons in the Peninsular and Waterloo campaigns of the Napoleonic Wars.

SURTEES OF THE RIFLES *by William Surtees*—A Soldier of the 95th (Rifles) in the Peninsular campaign of the Napoleonic Wars.

ENSIGN BELL IN THE PENINSULAR WAR *by George Bell*—The Experiences of a young British Soldier of the 34th Regiment 'The Cumberland Gentlemen' in the Napoleonic wars.

WITH THE LIGHT DIVISION *by John H. Cooke*—The Experiences of an Officer of the 43rd Light Infantry in the Peninsula and South of France During the Napoleonic Wars

NAPOLEON'S IMPERIAL GUARD: FROM MARENGO TO WATERLOO by *J. T. Headley*—This is the story of Napoleon's Imperial Guard from the bearskin caps of the grenadiers to the flamboyance of their mounted chasseurs, their principal characters and the men who commanded them.

BATTLES & SIEGES OF THE PENINSULAR WAR *by W. H. Fitchett*—Corunna, Busaco, Albuera, Ciudad Rodrigo, Badajos, Salamanca, San Sebastian & Others

AVAILABLE ONLINE AT **www.leonaur.com**
AND OTHER GOOD BOOK STORES

NAP-1

LEONAUR

ALSO FROM LEONAUR

AVAILABLE IN SOFTCOVER OR HARDCOVER WITH DUST JACKET

WELLINGTON AND THE PYRENEES CAMPAIGN VOLUME I: FROM VITORIA TO THE BIDASSOA *by F. C. Beatson*—The final phase of the campaign in the Iberian Peninsula.

WELLINGTON AND THE INVASION OF FRANCE VOLUME II: THE BIDASSOA TO THE BATTLE OF THE NIVELLE *by F. C. Beatson*—The second of Beatson's series on the fall of Revolutionary France published by Leonaur, the reader is once again taken into the centre of Wellington's strategic and tactical genius.

WELLINGTON AND THE FALL OF FRANCE VOLUME III: THE GAVES AND THE BATTLE OF ORTHEZ *by F. C. Beatson*—This final chapter of F. C. Beatson's brilliant trilogy shows the 'captain of the age' at his most inspired and makes all three books essential additions to any Peninsular War library.

NAVAL BATTLES OF THE NAPOLEONIC WARS *by W. H. Fitchett*—Cape St.Vincent, the Nile, Cadiz, Copenhagen, Trafalgar & Others

SERGEANT GUILLEMARD: THE MAN WHO SHOT NELSON? *by Robert Guillemard*—A Soldier of the Infantry of the French Army of Napoleon on Campaign Throughout Europe

WITH THE GUARDS ACROSS THE PYRENEES *by Robert Batty*—The Experiences of a British Officer of Wellington's Army During the Battles for the Fall of Napoleonic France, 1813.

A STAFF OFFICER IN THE PENINSULA *by E. W. Buckham*—An Officer of the British Staff Corps Cavalry During the Peninsula Campaign of the Napoleonic Wars

THE LEIPZIG CAMPAIGN: 1813—NAPOLEON AND THE "BATTLE OF THE NATIONS" *by F. N. Maude*—Colonel Maude's analysis of Napoleon's campaign of 1813.

BUGEAUD: A PACK WITH A BATON *by Thomas Robert Bugeaud*—The Early Campaigns of a Soldier of Napoleon's Army Who Would Become a Marshal of France.

TWO LEONAUR ORIGINALS

SERGEANT NICOL *by Daniel Nicol*—The Experiences of a Gordon Highlander During the Napoleonic Wars in Egypt, the Peninsula and France.

WATERLOO RECOLLECTIONS *by Frederick Llewellyn*—Rare First Hand Accounts, Letters, Reports and Retellings from the Campaign of 1815.

AVAILABLE ONLINE AT**www.leonaur.com**
AND OTHER GOOD BOOK STORES

NAP-2

www.ingramcontent.com/pod-product-compliance
Lightning Source LLC
Chambersburg PA
CBHW021102090426
42738CB00006B/462